Rob Fuquay

# THE PASSION PLAY
## Living the Story of Christ's Last Days

Abingdon Press / Nashville

THE PASSION PLAY
LIVING THE STORY OF CHRIST'S LAST DAYS

*Copyright © 2019 Abingdon Press*
*All rights reserved.*

**Library of Congress Cataloging-in-Publication
data has been requested.**

978-1-5018-8441-2

19 20 21 22 23 24 25 26 27 28—10 9 8 7 6 5 4 3 2 1
MANUFACTURED IN THE UNITED STATES OF AMERICA

# CONTENTS

# INTRODUCTION

# INTRODUCTION

All the world's a stage,
And all the men and women merely players;
They have their exits and their entrances,
And one man in his time plays many parts.

*William Shakespeare*
As You Like It *(Act II, Scene VII)*

It was 1632. After months of working as a farmhand in the neighboring Bavarian village of Eschenlohe, Kaspar Schisler finally made it home. He couldn't wait to be reunited with his family. He was also looking forward to the three-day festival celebrating the anniversary of the church's consecration in his town. This was a joyous time for all of Oberammergau, a tiny German village located in the Bavarian Alps just north of the Austrian border. The festival would provide a needed relief from the fear and apprehension that had seized the community in the recent months.

Europe was languishing in the middle of the Thirty Years War, a religious, political conflict in the Holy Roman Empire that was the result of fallout from the Protestant Reformation. It was one of the most brutal and destructive wars in history resulting in more than eight million deaths, or a little over a tenth of the continent's population. Germany bore the greatest brunt of the war with its inhabitants reduced by as much as 20 percent.[1] One of the lethal outcomes of the war was disease. Often referred to under the general label of "the plague," this was most likely the bubonic plague, a deadly, contagious disease. Starting in higher density populations where the disease spread quickly, it was carried outward as people traveled, often fleeing battles and hardship. The disease began with flu-like symptoms but soon manifested with a rash on the body and swelling of the lymph nodes.

While Oberammergau's remote location protected it from the war's violence, it could not isolate it from disease. As news trickled into the village reporting how the deathly sickness was creeping closer to their doors, panic started rising among the citizens. The town council hastily called a special meeting. Securing their borders was the logical response. The gates of the village would be kept closed with guards posted round the clock. Anyone entering the village without permission would be locked up. Those wishing to be granted entry would be quarantined for a period of time after which there would be an inspection for signs of the disease. Immediately, order and calm were restored as a sense of normalcy returned to Oberammergau. That is, until Mr. Schisler came home.

Sneaking past the guards by night, Kaspar Schisler went straight to his house. His delight at finally being home with his family, unnoticed by guards, was diminished somewhat by a nagging headache and fever. He had no way of knowing he carried the disease with him. By the next day, the secret was out—literally! His wife and children, unknowingly carrying the disease, continued interacting with people in the village.

4

Within days, Kaspar Schisler would be dead with his family showing signs of illness. Soon they would also die and many in the town would discover that their safeguards had failed.

By summer of 1633, eighty-four villagers of Oberammergau would succumb to the plague. Fear grew into delirium as the people desperately looked for hope and answers. As their traditions taught them, they turned to God. A prayer gathering was held in the Roman Catholic parish church, the same church whose anniversary celebration brought Kaspar Schisler home. The people prayed before a crucifix that still stands in the sanctuary today. They prayed for God to spare them from any more deaths, and their prayers were answered. There were no more deaths attributed to the plague in Oberammergau.

Either as a part of their original prayers or a later response to God's favor, the people made a vow to God that they would perform a passion play every ten years. Thus, on Pentecost Sunday, 1634, a tradition was born that has since made Oberammergau world famous.

In 2010, more than a half-million people descended upon Oberammergau to attend one of the 102 performances that occurred between May and October. Estimates are even higher for the next production in 2020. The Oberammergau *Passionsspiele* is the largest amateur production in the world. The cast is composed entirely of members of the town, nearly two thousand of its five thousand residents! The *Passionsspiele* Theatre seats five thousand, meaning that on the days of production, Oberammergau doubles in size.

Everyone in Oberammergau shares in the Passion Play. Hotel and shop owners, restaurant workers, and even local residents work together to serve the needs of hosting large numbers of guests. The play lasts for six hours with a three-hour meal break in the middle. This requires combined efforts of nearly every restaurant, hotel, and household to accommodate such large numbers.

Oberammergau has come to be defined by the Passion Play. This idea strikes at the aim of this book: to help the reader ask, What defines you? In the pages that follow, you will learn about the many rituals and features that surround this unique telling of Jesus' last days. I hope you will appreciate the significance of the Oberammergau Passion Play story and consider the Passion of Jesus from a new perspective. But what will make this book a spiritual treasure will be the way it brings you back to that question of what defines you.

Shakespeare wrote, "All the world's a stage and all the men and women merely players." We all have a part to play in life. We enter the stage at some point and then we exit. What we do with our part and how we play it is entirely up to us. In Oberammergau, life revolves around the part people play in telling God's great story of sacrificial love in Christ. This story represents God's care, hope, and passion for all humanity. Understanding our part in this story can be defining and redefining.

Each chapter ahead will consider numerous aspects of Oberammergau's tradition and relate that tradition to the Passion story of Jesus Christ. You will be invited to consider how that tradition or feature connects to your own story, your relationship to Christ, and your desire to know the part you play in this life. In fact, let's start with a few things we have already considered, beginning with Kaspar Schisler.

## Will the Real Kaspar Please Stand Up?

No doubt he thought he was fine when he entered the village that day. He may have had a few coughs here or there, but surely he would have known if he had been carrying a deadly disease, or so the thinking might have gone. After all, he wanted to be home with his family. Waiting through a quarantine would have stolen precious time, and by the time Kaspar Schisler realized he was the problem it was too late.

How true for all of us! We don't typically see ourselves as a problem until the evidence is undeniable. Maybe the hidden problem is anger or greed or a simple selfish desire to get our way. A few years ago, there was a terrible wildfire in Colorado that destroyed thousands of acres of land. Despite all the warnings and bans on open burning of any kind, a fire was started by, of all people, a Forest Service worker! When we see ourselves as the last person who could cause serious harm, we can believe the rules don't apply to us.

The focal point of the Passion Play is the cross of Christ, which attests to the truth that every person needs forgiveness. "All we like sheep have gone astray," said Isaiah (53:6)—a sentiment echoed by Paul in the letter to the Romans (3:23). This book would come up short in telling about the Passion story of Jesus and a community's tradition of telling that story if it fails to recognize the *reason* for the story. Oberammergau's pledge to put on a passion play began because of one person ignoring rules he naively thought did not apply to him.

We all have the potential to be a Kaspar Schisler. That doesn't mean we are bad people. It means we have the capacity to do bad things or careless things. This book will consider that reality, even looking at how the Passion Play itself was capable of producing some very bad outcomes. I hope you will see yourself in these dramas, in the people of Oberammergau, and in the Gospels and that you may come to a new appreciation of the meaning of Christ's cross in your life.

## Minimize Panic by Maximizing Praise

By the time eighty-four members of their community died, the people turned in desperation to God. They could have spent their energy venting and fuming about the person who caused the problem or calling for inquiries into the breakdown of their security procedures or just outright giving up and saying, "It's hopeless. We're doomed." Instead the people called for a prayer service in which they vowed to lift up the suffering of Christ.

As we will see, this vow was not unusual for the times. Passion plays at that time were popular throughout Europe and especially in Bavarian villages. Vowing to put on a passion play was not unusual, but what stands out are the conditions in which they made such a vow. In a time of panic, they contemplated a way to praise God. Maybe the people were bargaining with God. As the old saying goes, "There are no atheists in foxholes." When we are desperate, we will do anything if God will give us relief.

The Oberammergau pledge was not just an immediate bargain. It was a vow to tell about Jesus' passion to future generations. Once every ten years meant that the ones who made the vow might only have a few productions in their lifetimes. They asked God to spare their lives for the sake of future generations.

Turning to God in a crisis might not immediately change the crisis, just as the villagers' vow didn't bring back to life eighty-four of their members. It can, however, change how we face a crisis, and depending on the vows we make, give us understanding of how God can work through a crisis and bring a new sense of our own purpose and place in life.

In each of the chapters ahead we will look at various aspects of the story of Jesus' passion as told by Oberammergauers for nearly four hundred years and consider our own story and the part God calls us to play in his story of love and redemption. God has a role for every person to play and every day is a new act in the drama.

## Do What Lies Within You

One last thought concerns a popular saying in the time of medieval European Christianity: "Do what lies within you." The idea was meant to convey an understanding of grace to people who wanted to know what they had to do to get into heaven. If we do our best to love and obey God, then God will accept us. Martin Luther, the Protestant Reformation leader who lived a century before Oberammergau began performing its play, wrestled with this idea. For him the saying was problematic, because he was never sure if he did all he could to merit God's love. This struggle led to one of the banner themes of the Reformation: *Sola Gratia*, or Grace Alone.

Yet, despite Luther's wrestling with the idea, consider possible meaning in the idea of doing what lies within you. It means we don't serve God to be loved by God. We serve God as a response to God's love. God neither expects nor desires from us things beyond our ability. God gives to each of us gifts and talents to use. All that is expected is for us to do what lies within us. Use the gifts we've got to honor God.

This is what the people of Oberammergau have been doing for four hundred years. They honor God with who they are and what they have. They don't let the idea that they aren't good enough to be on stage keep them from living the story of Jesus' passion. They allow that story to be told through them. Living this way is what the Christian life is all about.

The hope of this book is that you will see your imperfect life and amateur abilities as the very vehicles through which God desires to tell the story of his amazing love.

So let's take our seats. The stage is set. The curtains are opening. Let the story begin.

# CHAPTER 1

## THE POWER OF A VOW

# Chapter 1

# THE POWER OF A VOW

The plague did end in Oberammergau and many were
spared, which should please anyone who honestly
believes in the power of a vow.

*From the 1984 Passion Play Guidebook*

My life is defined by vows.

My parents stood at the altar of a Presbyterian church
in Hamilton, Ohio, on June 15, 1957, and exchanged vows
with the solemn pledge, "I do." That was a defining moment
for me since I was born nearly six years later. Soon after my
birth they presented me for baptism at the altar of a Methodist church in Winston-Salem, North Carolina, and vowed to
nurture me in the Christian faith and raise me in the church.
That vow led to my own decision fifteen years later to stand
at the altar of another Methodist congregation and accept
Christ as my Savior and become a full member of the church.
Eleven years later, I knelt at another altar as my bishop laid
hands on my head while saying, "Take thou authority to

preach the word," and I was ordained a United Methodist minister.

Within two years I would find myself standing at an altar in Dallas, Texas, vowing to take Susan as my wife. We presented all three of our daughters at altars for baptism and when they became teenagers, I laid my hands on each of their heads and confirmed them into the church.

As you can tell, altars and vows are a big part of my story. How big a part have they played in your story? How far back can you trace your family history and identify the people and the vows that determined that history? Are there moments in your family background when someone vowed to leave their home and travel to another country or region, and that is why you grew up where you did? Were there moments when someone vowed to adopt a faith or way of living that greatly impacted your life?

All of us have probably been defined by vows more than we know, but imagine growing up in a town where everyone who lives there has been shaped by the same vow made nearly four hundred years earlier. That is life in Oberammergau.

Every first year of a new decade, this sleepy little mountain village morphs into a production venue that welcomes the world to experience the *Passionsspiele*. The play, which lasts about six hours with a meal break in the middle, is performed more than one hundred times between mid-May and early October. Oberammergau has roughly five thousand residents. The theatre where the Passion Play is performed seats five thousand. In a performance year, Oberammergau welcomes more than a half-million people from all over the world.

The cast is made up of all ages of townspeople from babies to senior adults. To be in the cast, someone must have been born in Oberammergau or lived there at least twenty years. (However, this requirement is reduced to ten years if you married a native Oberammergauer.) Along with technicians, stagehands, costume and prop designers, it takes more than two thousand people to put on the play, or about 40 percent of the town's population. Even those without a direct role in the production share in the town's ability to carry off the large-scale performance. Every hotel is full. People serve as shuttle bus drivers and tour guides. All of the restaurants combined cannot accommodate the crowds during the meal break, so residents open their homes. It truly takes a village to put on the Passion Play in Oberammergau.

Why has this community gone to such effort for nearly four centuries? Because of a vow. By late 1633, eighty-four members of the town had died from the plague, a sizable percentage considering the population was about six hundred at the time. A meeting was called in the parish church for all citizens. They prayed before the crucifix that can still be seen in the church. They made the following vow: "Every ten years the devout representation of the sufferings and death of Christ should be given, so that God would have mercy and free our village from the appalling sickness."

The next year, in 1634, Oberammergau put on its first Passion Play on Pentecost Sunday on a stage in the cemetery built over the graves of the loved ones who had died in the plague.[1] Today the Oberammergau Passion Play is the longest running in the world and the only one that originated from a vow.[2]

The decision to honor God with a passion play versus building a chapel or monument is not unusual considering the times. Passion plays were popular throughout Europe and were a common way for a community to express its faith and devotion. The decision to offer the play just once a decade may reflect the size of production the people envisioned. This is just speculation, though, since we can't say for sure why the people chose what they did. What we do know is that the residents in Oberammergau today understand that the tradition started because their ancestors pleaded with God to spare them further deaths from the plague. There were no more deaths as a result of the disease after that prayer service.

Reflect for a moment on any times you have made similar vows to God. Have you ever been in a situation where you prayed, "God, if you'll get me out of this, I'll do anything for you"? We can all probably think of foolish predicaments where we made promises to God. I remember being at an amusement park when my kids were small. There was a roller coaster called "Kracken," which I assumed got its name because of the way your back feels after riding it. It didn't just go up and down; it went upside down and did corkscrews and flips all while dangling your body in the air. Halfway through the torture I prayed if God would let me survive without upchucking on everyone sitting behind me, I would never get on another roller coaster again. God came through.

Our vows can be trite if not downright selfish, and the less serious the situation, the less serious we are about keeping our promise. It's like the story of the man looking for a parking space. He prayed, "God, if you will open up a spot near the front I'll start going to church." Just then a car backed out of the very first space. He pulled in and said, "Don't worry, Lord, I just found one."

Sometimes our vows and follow-through are trivial. Once we have life under control on our terms, we don't need God's help. But then there are other times, times when the chances of our getting control are nonexistent. The medical results show you might have a potentially fatal disease. Your child faces a life-threatening surgery. Your spouse leaves you. Your job has been eliminated. An intruder points a gun at you.

For many of us, we don't make God all we need until God is all we've got. The people of Oberammergau turned to God because God was all they had. Without a miraculous intervention, they saw no hope for the future. Therefore, they made a vow, if God would spare them, they would honor God with a decennial passion play. Since God came through, now it was the people's turn.

## Bargaining with God?

Some find this part of the Oberammergau story troubling. The vow feels like a bargain with God. If God does something for them, they will do something for God. Genuine faith, goes the argument, means putting God first without conditions. Is a vow, like the one the people in Oberammergau made, a true sign of faith or simply an attempt to bribe God into acting on our behalf?

Let's consider two examples from the Old Testament. The first is Jacob, someone who knew a lot about trickery. He tricked his desperately hungry twin brother, Esau, into giving up his birthright for food Jacob had prepared. Some might say Jacob wasn't being underhanded, just smart. If his brother was willing to forgo his birthright for something of much lesser value, why should Jacob be blamed for obliging him?

On another occasion, however, Jacob was much more devious. Knowing his father, Isaac, didn't have long to live and his eyesight was failing, Jacob dressed up to appear and even smell like his brother in order to trick Isaac into giving him Esau's blessing. Now Jacobmay have been prompted by his mother, but his decision to comply serves as a reminder that all of us are responsible for our choices. We begin to see how telling Jacob's own birth was; he came into the world clutching the heel of his brother, symbolic of his attempt to grab everything his brother would one day have.

Jacob's actions caught up to him when Esau decided to take revenge. Fearing for his life his mother insisted Jacob travel to her homeland some distance away. En route, he stopped at a place he named Bethel to spend the night. In a dream he saw angels ascending and descending a ladder from heaven. God spoke to Jacob and informed him of the covenant sworn to his grandfather, Abraham, and father, Isaac. Jacob would continue that same promise to establish a great nation that would be holy to God. They would possess the land and be greatly blessed and bless the nations of the world.

When Jacob woke up, he built an altar and made this vow:

> *If God will be with me, and will keep me in this way that I go, and will give me bread to eat and clothing to wear, so that I come again to my father's house in peace, then the LORD shall be my God, and this stone, which I have set up for a pillar, shall be God's house; and of all that you give me I will surely give one-tenth to you.*
>
> *Genesis 28:20-22*

Does that feel a little conditional to you? Okay, maybe a lot conditional!

The second example is a woman named Hannah who lived roughly seven hundred years after Jacob. She wasn't on the run from anybody, but she had a difficult life since she was unable to have a child. However, she remained faithful to God.

One day while praying in the sanctuary in Shiloh she made a vow:

> *O LORD of hosts, if only you will look on the misery of your servant, and remember me, and not forget your servant, but will give to your servant a male child, then I will set him before you as a nazirite until the day of his death. He shall drink neither wine nor intoxicants, and no razor shall touch his head.*
>
> *1 Samuel 1:11*

Now perhaps Hannah's vow is less aggrandizing than Jacob's. After all, she wasn't just vowing to give a tenth of her income but her very own son. She pledged that he would be devoted completely to serve in the temple and be raised by the priest. Even so, on the surface, both vows come off as attempts to bargain with God. They have a quid pro quo quality about them. "Do *this* for me, God, and I'll do *that* for you." Of course, it's preposterous to think we have anything God so desperately needs that we can force God to act on our behalf. When it comes to our relationship with God, we are the needy ones. So how are we to understand these vows?

Typically, when we bargain, we bring something to the table. We bring what we hope someone else wants so we can get what we need. However, in both of these instances Jacob and Hannah possessed little material wealth. In fact, their "bargain" was what they would do with the blessing they hoped God would provide. They recognized what such a blessing would do for them personally: to provide material help in Jacob's case and to provide a child in Hannah's, but rather than being a bargain their vows were a declaration of obedience. If God should so favor them, they would be faithful in their response. They were simply promising to honor

God in advance, which is a powerful thing provided we come through on our end. And vows are not simply the province of Old Testament times; we see Paul completing a vow by cutting his hair in Acts 18:18.

When I was a pastor in North Carolina I was privileged to serve on the board of the Reynolds Program in Church Leadership. This program provided top quality leadership development for clergy comparable to the kinds of training top companies provide their executives. It was named for the benefactor, Royce Reynolds, who donated the funds to launch the program. Royce sold cars all of his career. By the end of it he owned more than a dozen dealerships in Greensboro, North Carolina. He used his wealth to start not only programs like this one but also many others that benefited local churches, various charities, global mission agencies, and his own congregation.

Royce did not come from a wealthy background, which is exactly why he became so generous. He grew up "dirt poor," as he says, in rural Alabama. Early in his marriage and career, he was struggling to make ends meet. One day as he was walking down a road, he fell to his knees and prayed. He told the Lord he needed a spiritual partner who would share in his success and vowed to give ten percent of everything he made.

Soon after, his sales job really picked up. He took a check for a tithe of his income to give to the pastor of his church. The pastor, who knew Royce's financial condition, asked if he could afford to give that much. Royce said, "I told him he didn't understand. I have to pay off my partner. That is his share. That is how my stewardship began."[3]

Later he moved to North Carolina and bought his own

struggling Pontiac dealership that took off and allowed him to open numerous other dealerships. All along the way he was true to his promise. He gave generously to God. Royce has given away millions of dollars in his life and credits God for everything. He cites the vow he made as a young man at the start of his career. He didn't bargain with God. He just made God a promise of what he would do if God should bless him.

Isn't that what a vow is after all—promising what we will do in advance?

I believe this is what the people in Oberammergau did in 1633. Were they desperate? Absolutely. They lost nearly one in seven people to the plague. Were they devout? Their history of celebrating holy occasions was evidence, but so was their surrender to God in crisis. Clearly, they had more than a fair-weather faith. But their most important characteristic was their seriousness. They made a vow they had no possibility of fulfilling unless God intervened. Without God's answer to their prayer they had no future with which to carry out the promise of performing a passion play for generations to come. They were completely serious about giving to God what only God could give to them.

## Never Forget

One curiosity about the vow is just when it was made. Records from the actual period are scant. Priests typically were the historians in small villages and consistency of record keeping varied from priest to priest. Archives show that the deaths of people from the plague ranged from November 1632 to July 1633, but the traditional date given the vow is October 28, 1633, a full three months after the last recorded death. The longest period between deaths up to that point was no more than a few weeks. It seems odd that they would have waited three months with no reported fatalities after eight straight months of funerals before calling for a prayer service.

One explanation might simply be inaccuracy in the dates. Perhaps the vow occurred in July. Some historians look at various references to prove that is more likely. However, another possibility is that the October date might not have been the only prayer meeting of the people. They may have gathered in July to pray for relief and discuss what they would do as a community if God answered their prayer. Some months later, in October, realizing God had answered their prayers, they returned to officially vow their dedication to carry out this promise.

Whether or not that is true, this possibility points out a truth. We recognize God's active hand with the perspective of time and distance. Sometimes we sense God's movement in the present, but very often we understand God's involvement in retrospect. As my preaching professor in seminary, Dr. Fred Craddock, used to say, faith is less about a blind trust in an unknown future as it is a claim that God has been working in our known past. Recognizing that favorable turns of events, good fortune, and coincidences are actually God's blessing is an act of faith. I can imagine some villager in Oberammergau who was present when the people prayed in a crisis saying later, "Remember when we prayed that night? Well, God came through! God has spared us! We must now follow through on our vow."

Can you remember any past experiences when you prayed for God to get you through a tough situation, and now, with time and distance, you can see that God acted? Have you ever been tempted to forget promises you made to God in a crisis once the crisis was averted? If so, know that these are not salvation issues. God doesn't bar us from heaven because we didn't uphold a pledge we made. However, I do like the idea that it's never too late to be faithful.

## The Power of a Vow Fulfilled

Let's think about the power of fulfilling vows by distinguishing between vows and oaths. Oaths typically involve affairs of this world. Citizens swear an oath of allegiance. Doctors pledge the Hippocratic oath. Judges pledge an oath to administer justice. Presidents and government officials take an oath of office. Sometimes oaths are between two people promising to fulfill a pledge to each other.

Vows, on the other hand, involve God. Vows may be between two people, such as a marriage vow, but God is involved in the promise they make. Keeping a vow is a holy obedience. With this in mind, consider a few implications of maintaining a vow.

### Keeping a Vow Is a Response, Not a Prerequisite, to Grace

Since the beginning of my ministry, every fall I have led stewardship campaigns in the churches I serve. This provides an annual opportunity to renew our membership vows to support the church through our "prayers, presence, gifts, service, and witness." The campaign always ends with a Pledge Commitment Sunday when we will fill out cards pledging our support for the year ahead.

Inevitably there are people who don't pledge for fear of not living up to their commitment. Particularly when it comes to their financial support, they say, "What if my job changes and my income goes down? What if I have an emergency and can't fulfill my pledge? A vow to God is a serious thing, so I don't pledge. I will be faithful with what I have."

In many ways that is understandable and commendable. It reflects a serious attitude about vows. But what would it mean if we stood at the altar and said the same to our spouse? "I will be faithful with what I have. I'll do my best." Perhaps the end result still means the same, but how much more powerful is it to hear from someone you love, "I do. I will!"

God doesn't expect us to be faithful beyond our means. As Paul said, "God will accept your gift on the basis of what you have, not on what you don't have" (2 Corinthians 8:12 GNT). Not pledging to God for fear of repercussion if we miss a payment turns God into little more than a loan officer. The fact is, God doesn't loan to us. God gives freely. Our vows to God are responses to God's blessing, not prerequisites for receiving.

When we make a vow, it comes out of love and gratitude for all God has done. We aren't earning brownie points with God. We aren't bargaining for future reward. We vow because we realize that without God, we would not have anything to vow in the first place.

Some residents in Oberammergau today are descendants of original cast members in the *Passionsspiele* of 1634. Had those loved ones died in the plague these descendants wouldn't be here today. God's answer to the prayers of their ancestors means they have a reason and opportunity to keep that tradition going.

What are reasons you have to make vows to God? Are there miraculous events in your history without which you wouldn't be here today? Our vows are always responses to God's grace.

### A Vow Gives Us Something to Live Up To

In part 1 of The Lord of the Rings trilogy, *The Fellowship of the Ring*, Frodo recognizes the risk he has brought to those who have promised to travel with him to destroy the ring on Mount Doom. He decides to go alone. He gets into a boat and begins crossing a lake when his friend Sam reaches the shore and begs Frodo to come back. When he doesn't, Sam jumps into the water even though he can't swim. He goes under and is about to drown when Frodo yanks him up and into the boat. Sam looks up at him and says, "I made a promise, Mr. Frodo. A promise! 'Don't you leave him, Samwise Gamgee.' And I don't mean to! I don't mean to!"[4]

That scene still gets me. A promise, like a vow, is a powerful thing. A promise can cause us to do things we never would have otherwise. A promise brings something out of us, something good and big and demanding. A promise like that gives us a reason to live.

Psychiatrist Viktor Frankl observed this in a Nazi concentration camp. The prisoners who survived were ones who found a reason to live, whether it was helping other inmates or getting back to a cause that consumed them before they were imprisoned. For Frankl, his reason to live became taking what he observed and learned in the camp to benefit others in the future.

There is something about a vow that imbeds a sense of *why* within us. A woman I knew in a previous church I served didn't go through with a plan to take her life because of a promise she made. A failed marriage and a gambling addiction had robbed her of hope. She decided to take her life, but the one thing that kept her from pulling the trigger of a pistol was remembering a promise she made to her niece to visit her church with her. She laid down the pistol until she at least fulfilled that promise. What she didn't factor into her thinking was the injection of hope she would find as she kept her promise. She sat through the first Sunday with tears in her eyes feeling that God was speaking directly to her. She returned for a second week and before long she made the decision to keep living. Today she is a happy woman who has found love and joy again in her life. This story brings us hope that even those whose desperation leads them downward may find their way to the surface.

What vows have you made that give you a reason to live? Who in your life depends on you? You never know when a promise we have no desire to keep will be the very thing God uses to give us a new future.

### Our Vows Are Bigger Than Us

One final thought as we close this first chapter. Our vows to God impact more than just our own lives. Our middle daughter, Sarah, is the director of Project Transformation Indianapolis, a literacy development program helping at-risk children. I attended the celebration event at the end of her pilot year. Kids spoke and sang about what the program meant to them.

Someone came up behind me and said, "You have to feel good seeing what you've been a part of." I quickly said, "Oh no, I can't take any credit. This is the work of my daughter and her team." The person said, "Hear me out. You and Susan made a vow at an altar and as a result your daughter was born.

Plus, you vowed to raise and nurture her in the faith when she was baptized. Don't you think God used that nurturing to guide her to do what she's doing?" I still wasn't prepared to take any credit, but there was an idea in this person's words I couldn't debate. God takes our vows and does more with them than we can know or sometimes foresee.

When the villagers of Oberammergau made a vow in 1633, they were most likely thinking of their own commitment. Surely, they had no way of knowing how a prayer meeting one night would shape the lives of generations to come. Vows have that kind of power. God uses the promises people make to impact others far beyond the knowing and even intention of the promise-makers.

Victor Hugo described this most powerfully in the main character of *Les Misérables*. Jean Valjean was a released convict in eighteenth-century France. Turned away by people, he ends up in the home of a bishop who gives him supper and a warm bed. During the night Valjean awakens and decides to steal the bishop's silver forks and knives, but the next day he is caught and brought back to the bishop.

Shocking to everyone, but especially Jean Valjean, the bishop gladly greets him, explaining that he forgot the silver candlesticks. "Do not forget, never forget, that you have promised to use this money in becoming an honest man . . . Jean Valjean, my brother, you no longer belong to evil, but to good. It is your soul that I buy from you; I withdraw it from black thoughts and perdition, and I give it to God."[5]

Valjean eventually settles in a distant community and assumes a new name. His generosity and sacrifices earn him the reputation of being a saint. He eventually takes in a young girl whose mother has died and adopts the girl as his own daughter. Valjean never remembered actually promising to use the bishop's gifts to be an honest man, but along the way he chose to make the promise his own, and many lives were the better for it. Hugo writes the story not because it actually happened but to inspire what can happen when we see our life as defined by a vow.

# CHAPTER 2

## THE IMPORTANCE OF COMMUNITY

# Chapter 2

# THE IMPORTANCE OF COMMUNITY

On Pentecost 1634, the people of Oberammergau
performed 'The Play about the Suffering, Death, and
Resurrection of our Lord Jesus Christ' for the first
time on a stage set up in the cemetery over the fresh
graves of the plague victims.

*From the Service Program Affirming*
*the Community's Vow 2018*

Think back on the happiest moments in your life. How
many of them involved other people? What about the pictures
on your refrigerator or the background of your computer or
phone? How many are images of people? Most of our cherished memories involve others.

When something really exciting or funny happens are you
quick to call or text someone? Now that my daughters are

getting settled on their own, my wife and I frequently receive text pictures showing off a new dress or a special meal at a restaurant. Whenever one of our teams wins a big game, we immediately call each other. Special times are made even better when we can share them.

Relationships are what matter most in life. When actress Sophia Loren once cried to her director, Vittorio De Sica, over jewelry that was stolen from her, he advised, "Never cry over anything that can't cry over you."[1] Sound wisdom. As Paul said, "Rejoice with those who rejoice, weep with those who weep" (Romans 12:15). Having people to laugh and cry with makes life worth living. The experience of genuine community is a sacred gift.

I experienced something of this gift on a crisp fall Saturday morning in Oberammergau. Many there would claim this day as the most special in the life of the town, and it wasn't even during the Passion Play year! Instead it was nineteen months prior to the first performance of the next running of the play. Those years are special for people visiting Oberammergau, but this day was special for those who live there.

I could feel the anticipation in the air as camera crews started setting up outside the Passion Play Theatre. Not too far away hundreds of people had gathered at the parish church for an opening worship service. From there a procession formed behind religious and civic leaders, bands and choirs, as they made their way to the Lutheran church. Prayers were spoken from the steps, then everyone walked the short distance to the Passion Play Theatre where hundreds more had arrived to enter with them.

Inside, another service was conducted and broadcast on national television. Names of some of the original villagers who died in the plague were read. The people reaffirmed their ancient vow and sang the hymn "Heil dir, Heil dir, O Davids Sohn!" No one needed to look down at the words: "Hail to Thee! Hail to Thee! O David's son." This is Oberammergau's anthem.

Once concluded, the multitude spilled outside to the courtyard in front of the theatre where even more of the town's population waited. They faced a giant chalkboard listing the main characters in the play with blank spaces beside each. An age-old ritual was about to take place: the naming of the cast. People have waited a decade to see who will get the primary roles.

Before starting, the director speaks to the crowd. He recognizes the man who retired from writing the names after fifty years, which was just five times! For the very first time a girl will write the names. The director also points out that the coming Passion Play will be the first to have more women than men in the cast and that the older ones need to accept lesser roles to make room for younger ones. "We must keep involving our youth," he passionately pleads, "so that the play has a future!"

The girl begins writing the first name, Frederik Mayet. He has been chosen to play Jesus for the second time, not a common honor. She gets no further than the second letter and applause breaks out. Mayet is standing close to me and I see tears well up in his eyes as he sees his name appear for what is most likely the last time as Jesus.

His understudy is the next name written, Rochus Ruckel, the second youngest actor to play Jesus in the play's history. With each subsequent character, the crowd cheers as they recognize who is named. After all, these are their children, brothers, sisters, neighbors. All of the remaining primary cast members are eventually posted and people will spend the coming days inspecting the board. One man will be participating in his ninth Passion Play. Many names appear for the first time. The tradition lives on.

Oberammergau is clearly defined by the Passion Play and, on this occasion, I felt like a guest at a family reunion. A special history was remembered and imparted on a new generation. People were honored and celebrated. An entire village dedicated themselves again to a historic promise to God. This was a sacred day.

## Anything Worth Doing Is Worth Doing Right!

Right? At least that's the way I was taught. If something is worth doing, then it means giving your best. Do whatever that something is with excellence. Do it right. The problem is *right* doesn't require relationship. I find in my life the more I focus on being right the more I tend to isolate and push people away.

The truth is anything worth doing is worth doing with others. That doesn't make being right or excellent unimportant. It means really important tasks are meant to require the help of other people. If the only challenges we accept in life are ones we can do alone, we aren't living with a high enough bar. In Oberammergau it takes a village to fulfill their vow. A great cause always requires community.

Jesus himself demonstrates this truth. He came to be the living expression of God's will and way of life in this world. While Mark's Gospel consistently describes Jesus as going off by himself, it is also true that one of the first things he did was call people to help him carry out his assignment. Jesus' chosen way was to fulfill his mission through community. Luke 6:12-16 tells how Jesus prayed all night before choosing twelve persons to join him in his work. In fact, he designates them apostles. An *apostle* means "one who is sent." Apostles are people sent out to represent the one who called them. They have accepted an important responsibility.

Apostles are different from disciples, though we often use these titles interchangeably for the Twelve. Notice how Luke describes what happened, "When morning came, [Jesus] called his disciples to him and chose twelve of them" (6:13 NIV). Notice how there were more than twelve "disciples." The word *disciple* describes the many followers who came and went during Jesus' ministry. They were interested. They followed. Some probably stayed with him all the way to Jerusalem, but we know others did not. The Gospel of John records that after a particularly difficult teaching "many of his disciples turned back and no longer followed him" (John 6:66 NIV).

Being a disciple didn't require much. You could follow at will. When you no longer liked what you heard or grew weary of the demand, you could quit. Being an apostle, though, is a different matter. Disciples who become apostles have made a choice. They have been invited to represent Jesus and have said, "You can count on me."

How does one go from disciple to apostle? Through Christ-centered community. In the process of coming to know Jesus and each other, apostles are willing to go beyond just passive interest to active representation. In fact, note that the twelve disciples came to believe as a result of belonging. This makes for an important observation on the way Christian faith is developed. With the exception of Paul's experience, there is no concept of believing in the New Testament apart from community. We come to know and believe in Christ through relationship. One time I heard a pastor point out that we become Christian when we commit to Christ, and we become church members when we commit to other Christians. Great distinction, but the two are inseparable. Believing and belonging go together. However, if believing is so central to Christian faith, then what?

## Why Is Community So Hard?

That day in Oberammergau when the cast was announced, I sought an interview with the director, Christian Stückl, one of Germany's leading stage directors. He agreed but asked if we could do so the next day. So, Sunday morning I met him outside the theatre. As I approached, I could tell he was finishing a conversation with someone who didn't look very pleased. After that person walked away Christian said, "I chose all the people for the key roles. Yesterday was wonderful. Parents and family of people I selected thanked me. Today I'm hearing from everyone else." Even a Passion Play director gets an earful!

Why does there have to be conflict when you're trying to carry out a good cause? Have you ever asked that about your church? It's been said that where the Lord builds a house of prayer, the devil builds a chapel. Sometimes it feels like the more noble the effort, the greater the disagreements along the way. No matter how worthwhile the cause, our egos get involved.

If *we* think community is hard, though, imagine what it was like for the first apostles. In the Twelve, you had Simon the Zealot. Zealots radically opposed Rome's presence in Israel. There was also Levi (or Matthew), a tax collector, someone

36

who had supported Rome. Don't you think they had some interesting conversations? There were also James and John who were known as the "sons of thunder." No doubt they added to the fireworks. Judas Iscariot, possibly a Judean, was the only non-Galilean, causing some to wonder if his betrayal was a result of feeling like the lone outsider.

The first band of Christ-followers shows us that community was not easy. They nearly split over the question of who would have places of honor in Jesus' kingdom. They could be petty, jealous, and insecure, but they had this going for them: they stuck with Jesus and they stuck together.

Shortly after the tragic 2018 shooting at Marjory Stoneman Douglas High School in Parkland, Florida, I shared with our congregation that we need to address gun violence and what we can do to prevent such tragedies. We had just started a new sermon series using mountain climbing as a metaphor for discipleship. We gave out little carabiners reminding everyone how mountain climbers stay clipped to each other who in turn are clipped to a guide. We used them to symbolize our desire to stay connected to Christ and one another.

One man who is a strong gun rights advocate was stewing in the pew. He heard my words as a liberal attempt to limit gun rights and after the service he left determined not to return. He picked up a carabiner on his way out and put it in his pocket. Later that day when he changed clothes, he pulled out the carabiner and got to thinking, "I can leave the church, but what do I have to hold on to? I might not like what I hear, but I don't want to be unclipped." He came back to church and still comes every Sunday. He doesn't always like what he hears, but he has stuck with Jesus and Jesus' community. He's a terrific person and I admire him because, even though he has strong opinions, he seeks Jesus' guidance in the company of others.

Christian Stückl said there were times in the history of the Passion Play when the town wondered if they should let the tradition die. He remembers as a boy a huge divide that occurred between traditionalists and reformers. An attempt failed to replace the script that went back to 1860 with a more poetic and spectacular one last used in 1760.[2] The divisions became so sharp that the people would not speak to each other until they were on stage presenting the Passion story of Jesus. However, day after day of performing the story brought about a change in people. By the end of the season, they found a way to continue together.

The experience of authentic community is a challenge. There's an old saying that comes from the Cornish coastal region of England. One man says to a close friend, "I think the whole world has gone mad except for thee and me, and sometimes I'm not so sure about thee!" Studies today show how a growing number of people aren't so sure either. Three-fourths of Americans feel that incivility has risen to a crisis level in our country and 56 percent believe it will only get worse. Most blame it on the rhetoric of political leaders. Ninety percent of Americans say incivility leads to intimidation, cyberbullying, discrimination, and violence. Studies also show that the average person encounters incivility around seven times a week![3]

Do you ever feel we have so many twenty-four-hour news programs with so little new news? The same topics get debated for hours and sometimes days, and the debaters argue back and forth but do little listening and understanding of the others' opinions. It's like watching old Westerns where one cowboy pops up from behind rocks to fire at the other who ducks behind his rocks to reload. Then he pops to return fire and back and forth it goes. Surrender happens only when the ammunition runs out.

Christian community is meant to be different. It's meant to look like the first apostles, very different people with different opinions, but whose connection to each other is defined by their connection to Christ. That kind of community is worth fighting for.

## Community That's Worth the Effort

Let's think about one of the best-known apostles who was not part of the original Twelve, Paul. Who gave him that title? This is a much-debated point in the New Testament and seemingly one that became a touchy issue for Paul himself as he felt the need to defend his apostleship (1 Corinthians 9:1-2). Some of the qualifications of the Twelve applied to Paul. He had seen Jesus and agreed to be his representative. This along with the evidence of the Holy Spirit working through Paul apparently received the commendation of James, Peter, and John (Galatians 2:9).

But just when was Paul actually sent out? After coming to Antioch. That was a special community of Christians and, in fact, the place where the label *Christian* was first used (Acts 11:26). Many followers of Jesus ended up there because of the persecution started by Paul before his conversion to Christ. Barnabas was sent to Antioch to investigate the reports of an outbreak of Holy Spirit activity. Upon discovering an active community of believers in Antioch, Barnabas went and found Paul, who up to this point had done little more than preach. Paul was brought to Antioch to help lead the church. Now

imagine being some of the people in the community who suffered persecution by Saul or people whose loved ones were
persecuted by Saul. What must have been their reaction when
Barnabas introduced Paul!

Yet they welcomed him and more. They received his leadership and more. They sent him out as an apostle to start
churches elsewhere. I believe when Paul launched his missionary campaigns his aim was to start other "Antiochs." He
wanted to start communities where Christ's presence was real
and where people would experience a second chance just as he
may have perceived he had in the Antioch community. If you
look at the dating of events, Paul could have spent as much
as fourteen to seventeen years between his conversion and the
start of his first journey. In other words, he had roughly a
decade and a half to come to terms with the forgiveness and
calling of Jesus. But it was the experience of call *through community* that launched him.

Now this all sounds quite lovely. You picture Paul, Barnabas, and the rest of their band linking arms as they head off
to unknown places. Sure, they may have outward opposition,
but nothing could fray their internal union. Right? Uh, not
so much. By the end of the trip, Paul and Barnabas would
have such a contentious argument that they would separate.
The disagreement occurred over Mark, who abandoned them
midway through the first trip. When they planned a second
missionary journey Barnabas wanted to give Mark a second
chance, but Paul refused. Of all people, *Paul* refused someone
a second chance!

Again, community is hard! Why? Because Paul, like the
rest of us, was a sinner. We all have the capacity to be two-
faced, to assume the break we got is more deserving than

someone else's. We can be like Paul in allowing ego to cause us to demand our own way. But here is an important detail in the whole Paul-Mark saga, and to miss this little-known fact is to miss a wonderful subplot. At the end of Paul's second letter to Timothy he writes, "Get Mark and bring him with you for he is useful in my ministry" (2 Timothy 4:11). What? How did that happen? We can't say for sure, but surely something changed.

We have more than a dozen of Paul's letters in the New Testament but scholars believe Paul wrote many more that are now lost. Could one of those lost letters have been to Mark? Could Paul have experienced a change of heart, a change maybe even prompted by fellow Christians or an experience in Christian community? I can imagine Paul writing Mark and saying something like "My dear Mark, I want you to know how sorry I am for the things I said and did long ago. I understand how my words and actions could have hurt you deeply. You are a wonderful servant and if you should so find it in yourself to forgive a foolish old man, I would welcome the opportunity to receive your help." Again, that's pure speculation. What isn't speculation is that Paul one day said, "Bring Mark. I need him."

Do you have any "lost letters"? I'm not thinking about actual letters you have written but ones that need to be written. Have they been lost because you haven't yet shared them? Has God put on your heart something you did that hurt or offended someone else? Do you need to write them and not make excuses? Just recognize what you think their feelings could be and how you seek their forgiveness. Maybe your lost letter is not one of apology but yearning. You know there has been division and you long for your relationship to be restored. Maybe the lost letter isn't even that. It is simply a blessing to give. The wounds and distance are too great. Restoring a relationship is not in anyone's best interest, but you desire closure. Perhaps just writing to extend a blessing would help. Lastly, maybe the lost letter is to someone who is no longer living. Your letter is addressed to heaven. You need the healing that comes from expressing what is on your heart, then taking the letter outside and burning it. As the smoke floats upward you ask God to deliver your message.

## What Unity Looks Like

Brad Stevens is a member of my church. Before he became head coach of the Boston Celtics, he was at Butler University. During one practice he told the players they were going to run 17s, a dreaded sprint drill every basketball player loathes. They would run four each and be timed on their performance. They assumed this was a drill to see who was the fastest. After completion the results were handed to Coach Stevens. He stood before the panting players and threw the stats on the floor. He said, "I don't care how fast you can run 17s. I did this exercise to see if any of you would encourage another player to improve his time. Only two of you did." It was one of the more effective lessons on team unity.

Fred Rogers, of *Mister Rogers' Neighborhood*, received an honorary doctorate at Marquette University in 2001, the same year he retired. He began his address by saying that "in loving and appreciating our neighbor, we're participating in something truly sacred." Then he recalled an event from a Special Olympics in Seattle where a boy fell down while running a sprint. When the other sprinters heard his cry they all stopped, went back, tended to him, then took hands and crossed the finish line together. Rogers commented on how the crowd cheered for a prolonged time. Why? Rogers said because "deep down we know what matters in this life is much more than winning for ourselves. What really matters is helping others win, too, even if it means slowing down and changing our course now and then."[4]

The Messianic Secret refers to the way Jesus frequently commands people not to tell anyone about his power. This mainly happens in the Gospel of Mark. It's a rather baffling aspect of Jesus' ministry since he sent out his followers to tell about him and do acts of ministry as they experienced him doing. Why would Jesus want his messianic power downplayed? Perhaps because, as Mark may have experienced, too many people were willing to follow Jesus because of what he would do for them, and Jesus was looking for followers who would do for others. When people are committed to the good of others, focus on a Savior who gave his life for them, tolerate each other's failures, persist in the face of conflict, and are quick to ask forgiveness for their errors, then they become what the church was meant to be.

## The Local Church Is the Hope of the World

For all that is wrong with the church, its institutional aloofness, its hypocrisies and discrimination, there is still something about the church that when it gets it right is the hope of the world. The apostles demonstrated this. Jesus didn't pick them for their education. He didn't pick them for their holiness. Though they practiced the traditions that celebrated their Jewish identity, as found in Torah, they had their prejudices and selfishness. He didn't pick them for their power and influence. Most were fishermen who came from unpopular places and would have been considered nobodies by the somebodies of the world. Jesus picked them because of something he saw in them—perhaps devotion, willingness to trust, maybe even their compassion.

There is a peculiar scene in the beginning of John's Gospel where Philip tells Nathanael about Jesus from Nazareth who he believes to be the Messiah. Nathanael says, "Can anything good come from Nazareth?" In other words, how can a nobody be a somebody? When he approached Jesus, Jesus called him "an Israelite in whom there is no deceit." Nathanael, feeling this was an accurate assessment, wanted to know how Jesus knew him. Jesus said, "I saw you sitting under the fig tree." Nathanael replied, "You are the son of God" (John 1:46-49).

What was it about Jesus' observation of Nathanael under a fig tree that made Nathanael confess faith? This has puzzled people for a long time. It seems there was something about Jesus' knowledge that Nathanael felt was supernatural. Maybe there was an obstruction of view that should have prevented Jesus from seeing him. Many believe the fig tree was a place Nathanael went for prayer. But perhaps the reason Jesus engaged with him had nothing to do with the fig tree. It was the fact that Jesus knew Nathanael was a skeptic and still was willing to seek and find out for himself. Perhaps that is why Jesus called him and what he was looking for in all the apostles—not people who already know the truth but people who are willing to learn.

People willing to bring their questions more than their certainties, willing to be challenged and put in uncomfortable places, willing to stay connected to others with whom they disagree—this is a community through which Jesus will bring hope to the world. Paul's appeal to the church not to squabble in 1 Corinthians 1:10, to be "of the same mind," underscores the idea of community. Tod Bolsinger reflects on Paul's meaning in *Canoeing the Mountains*, "The same mind is more than thinking the same way, it is about common cause, common care and a shared commitment to look out for others."[5]

How would you describe an *apostolic spirit*—the attitude Jesus is looking for in someone who would represent him? What kind of person does Jesus use to extend his ministry? I, for one, believe talent, ability, and drive all matter, but I also know that those are not enough. I believe devotion is critical. A person must seek the help of the Holy Spirit. Yet as I study the Scriptures and the model of the disciples, it seems something more is still necessary—followers committed to each other. Jesus said, "By this everyone will know that you are my disciples, if you have love for one another" (John 13:35). Willingness to love as Jesus loved may just be the most important attribute for being an apostle.

Stan Copeland, senior pastor of Lovers Lane United Methodist Church in Dallas, Texas, tells how founding pastor, Dr. Tom R. Shipp, came to be a Methodist. Tom's mother died when he was five and so his father moved the children and their grandmother from New Mexico back to the family home in Missouri. This was the 1920s and life was hard. Tom's dad got a job working for the railroad and when Tom's grandmother died, the children went to live with other families.

Tom went to college following high school and in 1939 was able to attend the Uniting Conference of the Methodist Church in Kansas City. That's when the Methodist church came back together after dividing over the issue of slavery in the mid-1800s. One of the speakers at the conference was

John Mott, leader in international youth organizations and the YMCA and recipient of a Nobel Peace Prize. He said:

> Only as we thus transcend our denominational, party, national, and racial boundaries and barriers can we hope to fulfil the mandate of our Lord. . . . The time is ripe for a great and striking emphasis upon the Kingdom of God as preached by Jesus Christ—an emphasis which shall be truly relevant to present-day needs and conditions, which shall dominate all other considerations and incentives, and which shall become contagious and irresistible.[6]

Tom was so inspired he responded to a call to ministry. He helped start Lovers Lane United Methodist Church with a desire to create a church that was open and welcoming to all so they could experience the hope of Christ.

So how did Tom Shipp become a Methodist? When he was a boy and was sent to live with other families, he ended up in the home of a German farming family. The first evening after completing his chores he came to join the family— father, mother, and two children—at their dinner table. He sat down and the father said to him, "Boy, you can't eat with the family. There's no room for you here. When we finish our meal, you will be served at a little table on the porch, and your bed is in the barn." This was the pattern of life for a whole year.

One day he contacted his father and said he couldn't take it anymore, so arrangements were made to go to another German farming family, only this family was different. They welcomed him. He sat at the table for dinner. He stayed in the home. Then Sunday came and they all went to church, a Methodist church, the same church attended by the other family Tom had stayed with. I'll share the rest in Tom Shipp's own words:

> The first Sunday I attended church it was communion. The ushers directed people to the communion table. The family I was with insisted that I go with them. As I knelt down (to receive the elements) the man I had previously worked for knelt down beside me on my right, and the man for whom I was now working was at my left.
>
> The communion elements were served. And the man at my right for whom I had worked took my hand and held it just as I reached for the bread. I can still feel the tension. The man to my left was a German, and his face turned bright red. I can still hear the words that he said as he leaned forward, the preacher still holding the elements, not moving. He said to the man, "It's not your table!" There was a hush over the whole sanctuary. "It's not your table! It's not your table!"
>
> Finally, before matters came to blows, the man released his grip and I was allowed to take Holy Communion for the first time.[7]

Tom Shipp's goal as a pastor was to lead a church that acted like that second family. Their love transformed his life, and God used his life to transform untold numbers of others. It only takes a spark.

# CHAPTER 3

## THE ROLE OF RITUAL

# Chapter 3

# THE ROLE OF RITUAL

No native in the village can think about his life without thinking about the play. The play is a part of us. It
controls the rhythms of our life, like it or not.

*James Shapiro*

Every Ash Wednesday in years ending in nine the people
of Oberammergau cease doing certain things. The men quit
shaving and along with the women stop cutting their hair. It
isn't some kind of community protest, but rather the official
start of Passion Play preparation. Though the first performance
won't be for at least fourteen months, it will take that long for
their beards and hair to grow to conform with long-held views
about the appearance of first-century Jews. Everyone in town
looks forward to the start of this once-a-decade ritual, except
barbers and hair stylists.

So much of Oberammergau evidences the rituals that
have come to define the town. The buildings themselves are a
unique display of the Passion Play's tradition with stunningly

beautiful outdoor paintings, called *Lüftmalerei,* depicting biblical scenes from the Passion story as well as fairy tales and aspects of Bavarian life. Every August 24, villagers climb the shark fin–shaped peak called Kofel Mountain, to build a bonfire celebrating the birthday of Ludwig II, the Bavarian king who visited in 1871 and received a private performance of the play. As a former director once said, "The play is part of us. It controls the rhythms of our life, like it or not."[1]

In this chapter we explore the role of ritual. What are rituals that make up your life? Is there an order to the way you start your day? Do you have daily walks, exercise routines, or devotional patterns? What weekly rituals do you have? Worship? Family or date nights? Recreation or chore routines? How about any annual rituals? Celebrations? Holidays? Vacations?

You can probably create a lengthy list of responses to those questions, but what about once-a-decade rituals? Do you have any? At most the average person has just seven to ten decennial events in life. Think about the unique power of having traditions or rituals that might get celebrated just a handful of times, or even just once, in your lifetime. The ancient Jews understood the power of ritual. Weekly Sabbath observance was a holy day when you did no work. Then there were Sabbath years, once every seven, when you did not plant in order to give the fields a rest. And then there was a Jubilee year, once every fifty, or sort of a Sabbath of Sabbath years. In these years, property got returned to original owners, slaves were set free, and debts were forgiven.

What would it look like to have Sabbath of Sabbaths or Jubilee year rituals? What would be some once-a-decade or once-in-a-lifetime events? Perhaps that would include the big birthdays or anniversaries that end in zero. What kind of rituals could accompany those? Maybe keeping a time capsule in which you renew and update the important vows of your life. Maybe that is where you keep a journal in which you celebrate those special days by recording what defines the past ten years and what you look forward to in the years ahead. What would it mean to have a once-in-a-lifetime celebration? How might it be marked?

Rituals are the couplings that hold together our past and our future.

## The Art of Remembering

The owner of the hotel where I stayed in Oberammergau is a mother of two teenagers. The next play will be her seventh, though she is far from seventy years old. Added performances during the decades of the 1970s and 1980s meant she was in three plays by the time she finished high school. She explained that her children can't wait to escape Oberammergau. "This place is too small!" they complain. She remembers saying the same thing to her parents when she was an adolescent. She couldn't wait to leave and get out into the world. "But," she says, "when you are from Oberammergau it is a hard place to leave. You find yourself missing the traditions and history. I'm sure one day my kids will want to come back and sing the hymn with the people and take their place. They will remember who they are."

Her words reminded me of a quote by the Roman Catholic writer Flannery O'Connor, who was from Milledgeville, Georgia. She had traveled to New York City to receive a prize for one of her books. At a cocktail party in her honor she observed and listened to the literary connoisseurs and was overheard to say, "These people aren't from anywhere."

Knowing where we are from does a lot more than make us interesting people.

In 2010, researchers at Emory University in Atlanta published a study on the importance of children knowing their family history. They found that families who practiced rituals, such as dinnertime conversations in which knowledge of their past was shared, helped to deepen children's identity. The study found links between knowing family history and self-esteem and the ability to deal with the effects of stress. This led the researchers to create the DYK Scale, or Do You Know set of questions, to help families share their past. These questions include ones like: Do you know how your parents met? Do you know where your parents grew up? Do you know the source of your name?

The DYK Scale makes for some fun family exercises around a dinner table. Rituals invite us to remember something important about ourselves, such as who we are and where we are from. As Aristotle said, "We are what we repeatedly do." Such rituals as dinnertime conversations about our family shape our future beyond our understanding. Knowing people in our past who persevered through adversity gives us the hope that we can as well. Hearing about ancestors who immigrated or pioneered to new locations builds a courage in us.

Of course, the opposite holds true as well. Our family histories may include stories of failure and even embarrassment. Which stories we choose to tell about our family become the stories we tell about ourselves. We are in large part what we choose to remember. So, with that in mind, let's consider a very important dinner table where a most important ritual took place that has much to say about our future.

## A Table of Remembrance

Wandering behind the stage of the Passion Play Theatre, I walked into a room with a long, rustic wooden table. On top of it was a large menorah. A number of wooden plates and utensils were scattered across the table. In the center was a chalice. I realized *this* was the Communion table for the play. It was several hundred years old. It had been used in more than twenty productions, over half the life of the play itself.

Shapers of The Passion Play had chosen to adopt a more fifteenth-century da Vinci-style setting for this scene, imitating *The Last Supper* painting. Many historians say Jesus and the disciples were more likely at a triclinium table, a three-sided table with legs short enough so that people leaned against it while lying on the floor. The play may use the more popular image for practical reasons like allowing viewers to see all the actors. Regardless, this scene captures a most important moment in Jesus' ministry.

The Last Supper is a turning point. Everything before this scene involves a free Jesus. From now on the rest of Jesus' earthly ministry will be as a prisoner. This meal links these two divergent roles. Luke begins the ritual with this statement from Jesus, "I have eagerly desired to eat this Passover with you before I suffer" (Luke 22:15). Knowing what was ahead, the pain and loneliness he was about to face, Jesus needed the company of his closest companions sharing in a most important ritual.

The meal, of course, is not Holy Communion, but a Passover or Seder meal (in John's Gospel, the meal is *not* a Seder meal). *Seder* means "order" in Hebrew, and everything about this meal is grounded in order and ritual. In later tradition (not at the time of the Last Supper), the Seder meal became a very important occasion for Jewish people as they celebrated as a family in the home. The youngest child begins the ritual by asking, "Why is this night different from all other nights?" Then the story is told. The Exodus is recalled. Bitter herbs remind everyone of the bitterness of slavery. The *charoset* is a fruit and nut mixture recalling Pharaoh's command that the Jews make bricks without straw. Parsley dipped in saltwater symbolizes the tears of the people. The shank bone of a lamb represents the sacrificial lambs whose blood was painted over the doorways so the angel of death would pass over every Hebrew home. A hard-boiled egg represents the hope of new life that God brings.

Pieces of matzah, or unleavened bread, will be used symbolically as the meal goes along. In modern Seder meals a piece of matzah is broken in half, wrapped in cloth, and hidden. This provides a fun activity for children who hunt for the missing matzah, but the symbolism is important. The missing piece represents our ongoing search for completeness in the world that we pray God will bring. At some point in the meal Jesus took a piece of the matzah and gave it to his disciples with the astonishing new interpretation that this bread now symbolizes his body. Afterward he took one of the symbolic cups of wine, representing the fulfillment of the prophet's promise, and said, "This is my blood . . . which is poured out for many." He offered both symbols with the words, "Do this in remembrance of me."

Through a meal that remembers God's power of deliverance, Jesus offers symbols by which to remember him. He knows he is about to leave the disciples and is aware of the crisis of faith about to happen to them. He also knows the limits of their flesh. They will need something to touch and hold as a reminder that God has a hold of them. As real as a cup in their hands and bread in their mouths, so is the reality of his forgiveness and promise never to leave or forsake them.

Throughout the Bible, God offers his children rituals to keep them focused and connected to God. God understands that we all need regular routines and practices to stay connected to the Eternal. So, let's broaden our thinking and consider the power of ritual in our own lives.

## The Power of Ritual

Ash Wednesday, the beginning of Lent, is loaded with practices of self-denial. Since Lent is a time to focus on the passion, or suffering, of Christ, many Christians identify things they will give up for the forty-day season. For example, there are several traditions that reportedly go back to German practices in the past, such as Christians who wanted to remove eggs and butter and lard for Lent would make pancakes the day before Ash Wednesday. This is where the tradition of eating pancakes on Fat Tuesday began. Another tradition has to do with pretzels, which come from the German word *brezel*—derived from the Latin for *arm*. Tubes of dough were twisted into forms resembling arms folded in prayer. Today Christians observe many self-denying rituals that start on Ash Wednesday. I suppose, therefore, it made sense to people in Oberammergau to add to their Ash Wednesday observance every ten years the tradition of giving up shaving and cutting hair. In fact, the mayor now issues the official Hair Decree on the Ash Wednesday of the preceding year of the Passion Play.

Life needs its rituals. For a moment, take that idea beyond the religious realm and consider how much of a creature of habit you are. Do you have any repeating patterns in your life?

Do you sit in the same seat at church? Do you have old clothes you keep wearing even though they're getting worn? Any routines before a special event? I once went to a football game with a church member who had season tickets. Though we had just eaten lunch before the game, he got up to buy a hot dog right before the national anthem because "it's tradition."

We are all creatures of habit who crave a sense of sameness and routine. But as the old saying goes, habits can make us or break us. There are good habits and bad ones. A habit to exercise is certainly better than a habit to smoke a cigarette. Habits can be formed intentionally and unintentionally, though experts say all habits have triggers. In his New York Times best seller, *The Power of Habit*, Charles Duhigg identifies three activities our brains process in a habit, which he calls the Habit Loop: a cue (or trigger), a routine, and a reward.[2] He illustrates with the experiment of a mouse that hears a click meaning a gate opens. The mouse comes to understand that going through the gate and following a certain path leads to cheese. So the cue is the click, the routine is the path, and the reward the cheese. All routines have these elements.

Duhigg makes the point that the first time the mouse hears the click, he is carefully sniffing his way along the path. Though he smells cheese, he isn't sure just how to get there. The brain is working overtime processing all kinds of information. After several routines, the mouse simply scurries straight to the cheese, no processing involved. This is what makes a habit, well, a habit. Whatever comes easy, without involving much brainpower, is what we will do.

Replay in your mind something you easily do by habit like backing a car out of the driveway. For anyone who has driven very long this activity doesn't require much effort, but for a beginning driver, lots of anxiety and effort go into this simple exercise. Eventually though, familiar routine makes such an event a habit that requires little effort.

We can't always control the cues that make us respond, but we can decide the rewards we want and therefore change the routines that get us there. Rituals are like routines that help us respond to triggers in life such as a fight with our spouse, a blowup at work, a sudden shock. These events can cause automatic responses that put us in search of a soothing, comfortable feeling. That reward is not bad, but the routine that gets us there can make all the difference.

Toward the end of the book Duhigg talks about the power of spiritual community in forming habits. He uses civil rights workers and Saddleback Church as examples. He's not spiritualizing his point. In fact, just the opposite. He notes with scientific evidence the way spiritual support helps shape the habits we want to have. Of the college students who signed up to work in the Mississippi Summer Project, not all who stated a religious conviction for going actually ended up doing so. But, "of those applicants who mentioned a religious orientation *and* belonged to a religious organization . . . every single one made the trip."[3] His point is that the social habits of a community help us behave in a desired way. His other example of Saddleback Church speaks to the power of spiritual community in personal transformation. When people surround themselves by habits of faith, said Pastor Rick Warren of Saddleback Church, they "follow Christ not because you've led them there, but because it's who they are."[4]

The ritual of active participation in a vital spiritual community helps us become our best selves.

## The Solace of Sameness

Athletes are notorious for their rituals. Michael Jordan used to wear his college shorts under his Chicago Bulls uniform every game for good luck. Before every baseball game Wade Boggs used to take batting practice exactly at 5:17 and run sprints at 7:17. He also wrote the Hebrew word *Chai* (living) in the dirt before each time at bat even though he isn't Jewish![5] These, of course, are perhaps more superstition than ritual, but what's important to note is what the ritual does for the person. There is a comfort in the routine.

Coaches talk endlessly about the power of ritual. Basketball players are encouraged to follow a consistent routine before shooting free throws. Golf coaches talk about forming good "muscle memory" to create dependable swinging rhythms. When my daughters were little, they learned the Suzuki method of playing violin. Before they ever learned to play a note, they were taught proper stance and pre-performance routines. Such techniques have a way of putting a person at ease so they can perform at their best.

Spiritual rituals do the same. Sometimes the rituals have great meaning and interest. But the power of a ritual is not found in the benefit of any one routine, but in the formation that happens over long patterns of repeated behavior. It is a long walk in the same direction.

One of my professors in seminary, Dr. Walt Lowe, describes the experience when he took the first steps of such a walk. I won't forget him telling about being in a very confused place in life as a young man. He was struggling with so much of the chaos and confusion in the volatility of the sixties. The Vietnam War was in full swing. Protests and demonstrations abounded, and a few personal traumas left him in desperate search for stability. In a time when all traditions and institutions were being abandoned, he wandered into an Episcopal church one day. He was immediately struck by a feeling of disconnection. The people were moving through this ritual while so much turmoil was happening outside, but he felt at peace. As he sat there that day, he realized that in this place there was order. There was no confusion. He found something he was desperately looking for. This was his entrance into the church.

Ritual provides a solace in connecting us to the God who brings order out of chaos, but there is one important caveat to consider.

## God Is Never Reduced to Ritual

One of the challenges presented by rituals is that they can take on the status of the One to whom they point. In other words, the rituals themselves can become the object of worship. Oberammergau has struggled with this reality through the years. Arguments over scripts and music reflect the efforts to make such elements sacrosanct. But the temptation is understandable. Anything that connects us to the sacred can become sacred for us.

My wife, Susan, tells about attending the Christmas Eve Communion Service at her home church when she was in college. Her dad had been the senior pastor at the church for ten years but left some months earlier after being elected bishop. Susan was missing the familiarity of home. Her first year of college was a challenging year of transition. She couldn't wait to get home for Christmas break and attend worship at her home church. Christmas Eve Communion was her favorite service of the year, but that year the new pastor made changes in the worship. Instead of coming to the altar for Communion, he had the elements passed in the pew. As insignificant as it sounds, this was an emotional experience for her. She was so desperate for a familiar, much anticipated ritual that connected her to God that this simple change left her feeling alone and detached.

She would later come to understand how important this experience was for her own faith development. Her need was God not the ritual. The ritual connected her to God, but that didn't mean God's connection to her was dependent on the ritual. She just needed to keep her focus on Christ.

Jesus said, "Do this in remembrance of me." The aim is to believe that Jesus continues to be as real for us now as in his earthly life. We aren't just doing rituals that remind us of what Jesus did, we are doing rituals that help us experience what Jesus is doing in our lives now and will do.

God is not reduced to ritual but stands beyond the symbols and practices that point to God. Ritual simply connects us to what we need most: the living, real presence of God in our lives.

## Rituals Help Us Find Our Way Home

There is something about a ritual frequently performed that gets inside of you like a song you can't get out of your head. Sometimes you get away from rituals. You may even rebel against them, but when you return you discover something in the rituals that are an inescapable part of you. A true spiritual ritual communicates the presence of God that makes us feel at home. A church I know hangs a sign over the door that says, "If you are here for the first time, Welcome Home."

Jim Harnish, founding pastor of St. Luke's United

Methodist Church in Orlando, Florida, tells about a Christmas Eve Sunday years ago when a rare freeze caused a power outage throughout central Florida. Though the attendance that morning was sparse, the service proceeded. As he followed the choir into the sanctuary, he noticed an elderly stranger sitting with Susie. Susie had recently returned to the faith and to the Methodist church in which she had been raised.

Her father was Harry Blackmun, a US Supreme Court justice appointed by President Nixon when Susie was in college. The move to Washington, along with Watergate, the Vietnam War, race riots, and all that accompanied the sixties and seventies sparked a rebellion in Susie. She left her faith and family. She often traveled, keeping little contact with her parents. Eventually she married and had a baby. The baby served to bring daughter and father together in a way only grandchildren can do. Faith remained the only divide. Her father was glad to have a relationship with his daughter again, though he had let go of hopes that she would return to church.

Susie, however, found she was missing something in life. Her family settled in Orlando and started attending church. This was her path back home.

While visiting that Christmas, Susie's father could not have been more shocked when his daughter asked if he wanted to attend worship with her that Sunday. That Sunday happened to be a Communion service and Pastor Harnish noticed that father and daughter lingered an extra-long time at the Communion rail. When Justice Blackmun rose, he wiped tears from his eyes. Gathered around a familiar table, father and daughter were fully home.

# CHAPTER 4

## LIVING THE STORY

# Chapter 4

# LIVING THE STORY

*When you are born in the village, it is in your blood.*
*Stefan Hageneier, Passion Play Stage Designer*

Recruiting starts young in Oberammergau. From the earliest school grades, teachers look for artistic ability. "She shows a dramatic flair." "He has technical abilities." "That one could be a wood-carver." Since there are no age requirements to be in the play, children are groomed for roles both on and off the stage. The Passion Play gives meaning to everyone's life in Oberammergau.

People in the town are fond of saying that you don't just act a certain role, you *are* the role. They say a person didn't play the part of Caiaphas, but rather, "he was Caiaphas." In 1990 when Christian Stückl was narrowly elected to be the new director of the Passion Play, nervous town leaders brought in Cardinal Friedrich Wetter to assure as much as possible that the play would not change. After reading the script and thinking about the people who would fill the roles he said,

"The person imitating Jesus doesn't act the part, he has to *be* Jesus. To act it is impossible."[1]

"Jesus" wouldn't need the cardinal's help to remind him of that expectation. Frederik Mayet, who played Jesus in 2010, talked about the responsibility he felt having this role. "Those of us in the play are normal people. We go to the pub. We have another beer and wonder if we should. But playing Jesus, people look at you, see something in you. And it's given me a different understanding."[2] Not many years ago indecent or immoral behavior (meaning actions deemed inappropriate by the standard bearers of the play) could jeopardize one's place. In 1950, Gabrielle Gropper, a talented actress, had been slated to play Mary until she was seen dancing with American soldiers. She was, instead, reassigned what must have seemed a more appropriate role as Mary Magdalene, whom tradition wrongly assigns as a harlot![3]

The people in the play are not professionals. They are ordinary citizens of the village, but the standards are very high.

## Just Playing a Part?

Recognizing that the Play's popularity and growth was bringing an expectation regarding the character of the performers, Joseph Daisenberger, the parish priest who created an important rewrite of the play's script in 1860, addressed the cast in 1870 saying, "You are called upon this year to take part in the fulfillment of a great and holy vow: you will, as it were, in some measure take part in the Apostolic office. . . . Let nothing go on either within or without the theater, in the streets, in your houses, or in the church, which can give occasion for offense. The eyes of many strangers will be fixed not only on the Play, but on ourselves."[4]

Right or wrong, being in the play brings with it a certain expectation of piety. Today those expectations are greatly reduced, but still they are there, and this thought deals with an important issue in faith: the temptation to let faith become a show.

The 2016 movie *All the Way* is about the first year of Lyndon B. Johnson's presidency as he advanced the controversial legislation of civil rights. In the 1964 Democratic Convention there were rumors of a walk out by the Georgia delegation. Johnson called the governor on the phone to persuade him to pressure his delegation to hold fast. Sensing the governor's wavering, Johnson said, "You need to make up your mind once-and-for-all, what kind of Christian are you? Are you a once-a-week fella or do you hold the word in your heart?"[5]

We need to regularly consider what kind of Christians we are. Jesus once told a parable that points out the distinction between *listening* and *living*. The person who not only hears Jesus' words but also does them is like a builder who constructs a house on rock. When storms come, the solid foundation keeps the house from washing away. On the other hand, the person who just listens but doesn't live out Jesus' teaching is like a foolish builder who raises a house on sand. When the storms come the house washes away. Jesus makes a connection between sustaining life's storms and seeking to incorporate our faith into daily living.

Many congregations today struggle to keep their youth interested and involved in church. In our congregation we notice the drop-off occurs soon after confirmation, a nine-month training for church membership that begins around age thirteen. This is also a period of life when other activities like sports tend to compete with church involvement. However, the disengagement stems from more than just busyness.

Living the story means allowing the faith to become more than just an activity we do. Faithful living means employing religious activities into the routines of daily life, and allowing that faith to guide our decisions and actions. Faith that makes a positive difference in our relationships, our ability to handle stress, and the way we treat strangers in addition to how we prioritize our finances and deal with other aspects of our daily lives is an appealing and sustaining faith.

## Righteous, Not Just Religious

I talked with the owner of the hotel where I stayed in Oberammergau about the effect of living among all the activities of the Passion Play. When I asked if the tradition of the Passion Play and her involvement in it had an impact on her faith, she said flatly, "Not really." I was somewhat taken aback by her matter-of-fact response. She recognized that for some people this may be the case but not for her family. Though they are Christian they don't go to church. She didn't show any hesitation or reluctance in speaking about this, but the longer I listened the more I understood that her lack of religious practice had to do with issues regarding the church.

Scandals plaguing the Roman Catholic Church in the last decade have had a significant impact on regions like Bavaria. Only about 7 percent of Oberammergau's population regularly attends worship. As I studied what seemed like an obvious disconnect between a town that proudly produces a Passion Play and its disengagement from the church, I came to understand reasons that actually resemble faith and spirituality.

In a 2010 New York Times interview, Frederik Mayet (who played Jesus in 2010) talked candidly about his disenchantment with the church after Pope Benedict XVI reinstated four excommunicated bishops, including one who denied the

Holocaust. He said, "I didn't want to be a member of a church that welcomed Holocaust deniers with open arms. The leaders should think less about hierarchies and institutions and more about Jesus and how to reach the people again."[6]

Such expressions are not apathetic toward faith, they just describe disappointment toward the church. And let's understand we aren't talking about just Catholicism here. Every church struggles with becoming too bureaucratic and self-preserving. Every church has, in varying degrees, caused wounds in people. As Paul wrote, "we have this treasure in clay jars" (2 Corinthians 4:7). The church very much is an earthly institution composed of and led by imperfect, sinful, human beings.

Certainly, Jesus did not intend to form an institution. After Peter confessed, "You are the Messiah, son of the living God" (Matthew 16:16), Jesus said, "On this rock I will build my church" (Matthew 16:18). The description more often used in the New Testament for church is "body of Christ." After Jesus said in the Gospel of John that if the temple were destroyed, he would rebuild it in three days, John adds, "He was speaking of the temple of his body" (2:22). Throughout his letters Paul speaks of our being members of the body of Christ.

Jesus didn't want to leave behind an organization but an *organism*. He calls the church to be his living body where the Holy Spirit empowers ordinary, even sinful people, to be Christ's hands and feet in the world. Reflecting on comments by the hotel owner and studying the statements of people in the play, I found that though they didn't claim to be religious, their words reflected a deep yearning for a church as Jesus intended.

Living the story of Jesus' passion is a call to be not only religious but also righteous. Righteousness is not self-righteousness. Self-righteousness is more about right-ness, and there is a big difference between right-ness and righteousness. Religion too often focuses on right-ness, possessing truth, living in accordance with rules, being right. Being right doesn't require much of us other than knowing and doing what the rules of faith allow or require.

*Righteousness* is altogether different. Relationships take priority over rules. Grace over governance. Love becomes the primary law. Righteousness is about being rightly aligned with God, much like a computer aligns the margins evenly on the screen. Righteousness is about God's work to line up God's way of life in our lives, a way that comes into view in the life of Jesus.

In the start of the Sermon on the Mount Jesus spoke words that must have sounded like a fatal blow to his listeners, "Unless your righteousness exceeds that of the scribes and Pharisees, you will never enter the kingdom of heaven" (Matthew 5:20). How does one respond to such a demand? The scribes and Pharisees were paragons of righteousness. They followed every rule believed necessary for entering the kingdom of God. Exceed that level? Too hard!

As Jesus' listeners would learn in the rest of the sermon, however, he adds to the commandments. Do not hold on to anger, do not live with lust. If you are slapped on the cheek, turn the other. Love your enemies and pray for those who persecute you. Jesus calls people to a higher righteousness, a righteousness that gets demonstrated in Jesus' own life.

What does it mean to you to live a righteous life?

## Playing Many Parts

Another interesting observation about the Passion Play is the various roles cast members portray across the decades. One of the women playing Mary used to play Mary Magda-

lene. One of the two people sharing the role of Joseph of Ari-
mathea (the one who asked Pilate for permission to take Jesus'
body for burial) was the previous Pilate. Herod was a former
angel. Judas was the previous John. Caiaphas was once Jesus!

What a wonderful illustration of a universal truth: none
of us is completely one or the other. We're all a mixture of
saint and sinner, apostle and apostate, victor and villain. There
is a story about Leonardo da Vinci's *Last Supper* painting.
He used real life models to paint each character starting with
Jesus. When he got to the last one, a prisoner was brought out
of jail to pose as Judas. Da Vinci didn't recognize him but later
discovered that before the man ran afoul of the law, he had
been the model for Jesus!

The power of the Passion story is not that there are clear
lines of distinction between good and bad characters. We are
meant to see ourselves in all of them. Judas was a disciple who
was thought trustworthy enough to keep the money but was
also capable of betraying Jesus. Peter boasted he would die
with Jesus if need be, but his courage failed him at a critical
moment. Even Pilate appeared as though he wanted to do
the right thing and release Jesus, but in the end, he washed
his hands of responsibility. This play doesn't tell us who they
were. It tells us who *we* are.

Adolf Eichmann was a notorious Nazi who helped create and carry out the Holocaust. He managed to escape to
South America after World War II where he lived in hiding
until being captured and sent to Israel. He was eventually tried
and executed, but in the trial the defense had to produce witnesses who actually saw Eichmann commit atrocities. One of
the witnesses was a man named Yehiel De-Nur. While giving
testimony and looking at Eichmann, who was sitting behind a

glass booth, De-Nur suddenly collapsed to the floor sobbing uncontrollably. For a while the courtroom was in an uproar.

Some years later De-Nur was interviewed on the television program *60 Minutes*. He was asked what happened. Was he overcome with memories or hate? De-Nur said no. Instead it was something very surprising. When he saw that Eichmann looked just like an ordinary human being like himself, he was overcome with fear because he realized that meant he was capable of doing the same thing.[7]

What a statement and what a recognition of human potential. Was De-Nur someone on the edge with inner demons rising to the surface? No more so than the rest of us. In fact, that is the significance of his remarks. A person whom it was so easy to picture as a monster now appeared as normal as De-Nur himself. If a normal person could do such things, what does that say about the rest of us?

When we have been wounded by others the natural temptation is to say we would never act that way. We would never stoop to such a level. We may even demonize our enemies and turn them into something other than human. But to see them as humans, to see ourselves in them, is a powerful if not frightening thing.

As an old saying goes, "We're never as bad as our worst critics conclude, and we're never as good as our biggest admirers claim." We each have aspects of godliness in us that can be undermined by our capacity to do evil. And we have goodness that offsets our worst days. While we might like to think such fixed and hard lines exist between these characteristics, people like Yehiel De-Nur recognized those lines are not as firm as we would like to think.

Living the story is not about being good enough. It is not

about getting to a tipping point where the scales land on the side of being worthy to play a part in God's story. We are each a mishmash of competing drives, ambitions, and desires. Some are good; others, not. Perhaps one of the most relatable things Paul ever wrote was when he said, "For I do not do the good I want, but the evil I do not want is what I do" (Romans 7:19). Who can't identify with Paul's bewilderment? Being all good with no bad is not an option. Desiring to do good in spite of the bad is the aim.

## Skateboard Angels

Looking for this higher nature is what gives the Oberammergau Passion Play a sense of mission. Christian Stückl, who wanted to be a priest as a boy, brings a pastor's heart to his directing. He believes the younger generation needs a spiritual influence, so he is passionate about casting as many young people as he can. "I go to the skateboarding half-pipe and say, 'You're an angel! You're an apostle!'" he said. "And they all say yes immediately."[8]

This whole matter of having unseemly characters within us has another side. We have inner angels just waiting to find expression and it usually takes someone calling that forth. Isn't this what Jesus did? He observed fishermen by the Sea of Galilee and said, in effect, "Hey, I see you fishing for people. You can change the world!" And they said yes immediately! He watched Levi and said, "Hey, you can change people's lives. Come with me." And he said yes immediately. The word *angel* means messenger. God usually sends messengers to call forth the angels in us.

I don't know where I would be without people who were angels in my life and called forth things I didn't see in myself.

A neighbor of mine when I was just fourteen told my mother, "That boy of yours will make a pastor one day." God used her words to plant something in me I thought was a silly if not unwanted idea at the time. A youth leader listening to me reflect on scripture said, "You have a gift for analogy. I can see you being a good communicator one day." When I was washing dishes in a cafeteria during college, the food service director approached me and said, "I've been asked to start a new restaurant. How about being my manager?" She said she saw leadership qualities in me.

Have there been people in your life who saw things in you that you didn't see in yourself? The good within us—and the good we can do in our lives—is often called forth by people whose words of insight and encouragement are anointed by God to shape us in profound ways. How have you been shaped for the better by the messages of people? As well, how can you shape others by your words? Who are people to whom you can be an angel? Are there folks who impress you with their compassion or leadership or wisdom or communication ability? It's easy to keep our thoughts to ourselves. What if you made a quick list of people you can imagine God using to do great things? Now, how might you communicate that message to them? Sit down with them over coffee? Send an e-mail? Write a letter? You may be just the messenger God wants to use to shape a life.

My friend Dr. Clarence Moore has been pastor of New Era Church in Indianapolis for twenty-nine years. During that time the church has grown from sixty to several thousand members. One key reason is the way he motivates and brings forth the best in people. A few years ago, a local school that serves some of the most at-risk population of children in the city came to Dr. Moore to ask if his church could provide an after-school program. The school was looking for help with the kids who tended to have the least support and assistance with their education.

Dr. Moore agreed and through volunteer tutors, started the program. As I walked with him through the classrooms one day, he explained to me how every child has experienced the violent death of a loved one. Their life experiences often cause them to act out at school. What they are doing in this program is rescuing kids and helping them discover their potential.

One example is a boy named Chris. He was a regular at the after-school program but one day was causing a lot of disturbance. Finally, one of the volunteer teachers took him aside and asked, "What's wrong, Chris?" No response.

She persisted. "Chris, you have so much ability. I believe in you, but you have to let me help you. What do you need?"

He looked up and said, "You know, if I had a tee, I believe that would help me."

"A tee? What do you mean a tee?" She asked.

"You know a tee. I need a tee." He answered pointing at the necklace she was wearing. "Like that," he said.

She felt the cross around her neck and realized what he was talking about. He associated the love and support the people at the after-school program showed him with the "tees" they all wore.

As Dr. Moore says, "The goal of the Christian life is not just to wear the cross but to bear the cross." When we allow the redeeming, hope-giving, grace-showing, sin-forgiving, life-transforming love of Christ to become real through us, we bear the cross and live the story.

## Where Is My Stage?

Next to the Passion Play, Oberammergau is best known for its wood-carvers. The art has been passed down through generations across many centuries. Farmers began wood carving as a way to occupy themselves during the long winters as well as provide some supplemental income. Realizing the popularity of their products, they began peddling them, some even discovering new careers. Carvers created long boards to which they could attach their carvings and carry them on their backs going from village to village. As reputation of the quality and craftsmanship of Oberammergau's wood carvings spread, some carvers traveled as far as St. Petersburg, Russia.

One wood-carver, who works out of a house that has been in his family for four hundred years, showed me the display of the hundreds of figures he's created. Nearly all of them are religious in nature, most being characters from the Passion Play. Visitors often spend time before the play begins, as well as during the intermission, wandering in the many wood-carving shops quaintly nestled between the hotels and buildings along the village's narrow streets. This is not just a pleasant way to spend time but to appreciate an art that has not been handed over to machines. Each delicate wrinkle on a face or crease in clothing has been carefully whittled by hand. In the center of the village is a beautiful building called the *Pilatushaus*, named for the ornate painting on the front walls depicting Jesus appearing before Pilate. Inside the house are displays telling the history of wood carving in Oberammergau and one can see and talk with carvers as they work. When I spoke with the wood-carver whose shop I visited, I asked if the items he made reflected his own faith. He was quick to say, "Of course! Everything gives glory to God." Clearly the performers in the play are not the only ones God uses to tell the story of Jesus' passion.

His words reminded me of Martin Luther's idea of the priesthood of all believers. The maid milking the cow and the farmer baling hay carry out ministry as much as the priest in church. Every ten years, farmers, homemakers, clerks, and constables put their work clothes aside to don the garbs of priests, apostles, Roman soldiers, and Jesus. They spend tremendous hours rehearsing through the long winter and spring leading up to the first performance, and then spend the next five months working half days before heading to the theatre to perform the play. These "amateurs" get on a stage that enables them to tell the story of Jesus' passion to the world.

The word *amateur* derives from the Latin *amator*, which means "lover." Rather than meaning unqualified, it refers to someone who loves what they do and does what they do with love. God isn't looking for professionals. As Michael Counsell repeats an old saying, "Noah's ark was built by amateurs, but the *Titanic* by professionals!"[9] God doesn't need super-gifted, elite-level talent in order to do great things. God just needs a loving heart. Mother Teresa is frequently quoted as saying, "Not all of us can do great things, but we can do small things with great love." God desires amateurs, people with great love through whom God's love is made real and known.

Paul says, "For I suppose that God has appointed us . . . that we would be a stage play for the universe" (1 Corinthians 4:9, Aramaic Bible in Plain English). God gives every Christ-follower a stage. Whatever you do in your life can become a platform for God to use. Your work. Your neighborhood involvement. Your exercise facility. The places where you shop. Your child's team that you coach. What are the stages in your life God can use to be an influence of love and hope in other people's lives? What does it mean to allow those places to become a platform for God to use?

There is a wonderful little short film called *Validation*.[10] It isn't a religious movie but it has a spiritual message. The story is about a guy who validates people's parking tickets. His booth is at the end of a dark corner in an underground garage. Everything about this location would say this young man must not have much going for him to have a job like this. But he didn't let the size of his spotlight determine the potential of his "stage."

He used the opportunity to notice people in unique ways. He would find something about every person and compliment them. Maybe the style of their hair or the way their coat draws out the color of their eyes or how their hat gives them a very distinguished look. What begins to happen is that people look forward to getting "validated." Long lines start forming as word spreads about the parking validation guy.

The owner of the parking deck learns about the lines and wonders what must be wrong. How could someone screw up a job like that? After all it doesn't take any talent to validate parking tickets. He goes to reprimand the person, but they have never met. As soon as he walks up the parking validation guy starts complimenting his suit. "Wow," he says, "That suit was made for you. I can tell you are someone important. I hope the people you work for appreciate you." The man's frown turns into a smile. He forgets why he came down there in the first place!

The movie makes a simple but wonderful point about the power of helping people feel validated. Anyone can do it. This is the message that has been entrusted to you and me. God wants every person to feel a God-given worth and value in this world. God wants for all of us to feel validated. When we let ourselves become the actors through whom that message gets shared, then all the world becomes a stage.

# CHAPTER 5

## TELLING A
## BETTER STORY

# Chapter 5

# TELLING A

# BETTER STORY

For a whole year people will only talk about your
story. Make it understandable, meaningful, human, so
the audience can really feel who Jesus was.

*Christian Stückl, Passion Play Director*

In 1934, Oberammergau staged a special three hundredth jubilee anniversary production of the Passion Play. Just four years after the previous performances much had changed in Germany and especially in Oberammergau's state of Bavaria. The previous year the German Reichstag, the parliament building in Berlin, had mysteriously burned to the ground. The appointed chancellor, Adolf Hitler, used this moment to declare a national emergency and establish his Nazi Party as the ruling government. Immediately the Nazis gained total control over the nation and started arresting political enemies, suspending organizations like labor unions, and outlawing other political parties. During 1934, Hitler ordered the executions of political leaders he feared could be threats to his leadership while merging the offices of party leader, head of state, and chief of government into one and giving himself the title *Führer*, a German word meaning "leader" or "guide."

These were uncertain times in Germany and throughout Europe. Hitler's rhetoric of creating a superior Aryan race and eliminating less desirable people like gypsies, Jews, and homosexuals was alarming to many. However, in regions like Bavaria where Hitler sowed the seeds of what became the National Socialist (or Nazi) Party, the reactions were different. There was optimism that Germany would finally remove the scars left from World War I, and Hitler's star power was rising to the level of demigod.

And so it was that in August of that year Hitler attended one of the Oberammergau performances. He had attended a 1930 performance but without the fanfare of his return in 1934. That year many questions surrounded the influence of the Nazis on the play. Munich artist Hermann Keimel was asked to create an image for publicity posters. He designed a sketch of a dark, bleeding hand of Christ on the cross. When presented in Berlin, Joseph Goebbels, head of the ministry of propaganda, disapproved because of the way it depicted weakness. Another artist was commissioned and a second design was created showing a glimmering plain cross towering over the beautiful mountains and village.[1] A top Nazi official was asked to become the play's patron. The selection of persons for the main roles was done under the supervision of Hermann Esser, a Hitler appointee, which may account for the high number of Nazi party members chosen for the main roles.[2] Jesus was played by Alois Lang, who was Christ in the 1930 production. Though he was not a Nazi at the time, he did join the party in 1938. Some say he was made to appear very strong and commanding while Judas was made to look dirty and despising. Hitler even approved the script as *reichswichtig*, or "of national importance for the Reich."

At a dinner in 1942 Hitler had this to say about the Oberammergau Passion Play:

> One of our most important tasks will be to save future generations from a similar political fate and to maintain forever watchful in them a knowledge of the menace of Jewry. It is vital that the Passion play be continued at Oberammergau; for never has the menace of Jewry been so convincingly portrayed as in this presentation of what happened in the times of the Romans. There, one sees in Pontius Pilate a Roman racially and intellectually so superior that he stands out like a firm, clean rock in the middle of the whole muck and mire of Jewry.[3]

In this chapter we look at what has been a long and tragic aspect not only of the Oberammergau Passion Play but of all passion plays: anti-Semitism.

## A Dark History

In 1965, the Second Vatican Council issued a statement called *Nostra Aetate*, meaning "in our time," to revise the Catholic Church's relationship to other religions. In this document the Council repudiates all forms of anti-Semitism, particularly the charge that provokes so much of the hatred toward Jews: *deicide* (meaning the murder of God). What inclined the Second Vatican Council to feel a need to issue such a statement? In part, it was the negative emotion generated by passion plays that interpreted the biblical texts as condemning Jews for the death of Jesus.

The most offensive and inflammatory line in the passion narrative is the so-called "blood curse." This is the statement shouted by the crowd at Jesus' trial in the Gospel of Matthew. Pilate was seeking to find a way to release Jesus, but the harder he tried the more he feared an uproar by the crowd. Finally, he washed his hands of the whole affair and told the people, "I am innocent of this man's blood; see to it yourselves." The people shouted back, "His blood be on us and on our children!" (Matthew 27:24, 25).

Pilate is made to appear innocent of wrongdoing as if he were bullied into crucifying Jesus. Of course, this doesn't line up with what is historically known about Pilate, who was defiant toward Jewish leadership and brutal in his treatment of them. Regardless, this line spoken by the crowd has been a key source of hostility toward Jews because they are made to appear responsible for Jesus' death.

Passion plays have their roots in the earliest periods of church history when the telling of Christ's passion was encouraged on Good Friday using a variety of liturgies that included music. Over time these presentations incorporated more drama. By the late Middle Ages, in regions like Germany, passion plays became very popular at Eastertime, leaning heavily toward the dramatic. Around the time of Oberammergau's vow there were upward of three hundred passion plays in the neighboring towns of the Bavarian and Tyrolese regions.

Because of the way these plays emphasized and even embellished the role of the Jews in Jesus' crucifixion, outbreaks of violence often occurred following these plays. For many Jews, Easter was a frightening time. Assaults on Jews led cities like

Freiburg in 1338 to stop allowing anti-Semitic scenes in passion plays. By the sixteenth century, the city of Rome out-
lawed passion plays altogether because they spawned attacks
on the Jewish ghettos, enclosures where Jews were confined
by order of Pope Paul IV.

Were anti-Semitic beliefs formed by passion plays or did
the plays simply give expression to already existing prejudices?
That's hard to say. Prejudices against Jews come as early as
the Gospel literature and the writings of the Church Fathers.
What we do know is that anti-Jewish bigotry has deep roots
in Germany. In the City Church in Wittenberg, where Martin Luther often preached, there is a frieze about fifteen feet
above the corner of an outside wall depicting Jews as pigs.
Martin Luther would have walked under this disgusting image
almost daily. Perhaps that cultural bias was behind one of his
own despicable attacks on the Jews, which he wrote in a 1543
pamphlet, *On the Jews and Their Lies.*

Prejudice often prospers from false narratives that get
passed down. Eventually the narratives are not even a matter
of bias, they simply become our truth. They are the way we
see the world and one another. Even the best of us can live
with false narratives. They explain our problems and provide
someone to blame. Instead of judging the individual merits of
a person we judge whole classes and races of people as being
legitimate or illegitimate because our accepted narrative says
it is so. The only way such incorrect views change is to begin
telling a better story.

## Telling a Better Story

Christian Stückl, the director since 1990, has been trying
to tell a better story through the Oberammergau Passion Play.

His motivation may, in part, come from his own narrative. In 1950 his father was barred from playing Jesus because he married a Protestant. Since taking over, Stückl has sought to free the play from the narrow, exclusive opinions that have limited and hurt the play.[4]

Until 1990 the only women who could be in the play had to be unmarried and under thirty-five years of age. To change that Stückl had to go to high court in Munich. Then, in 2010, Stückl gave the role of Judas to Carlsten Luck, the first ever Protestant to be in the play. He has also made the play inclusive of Jews and Muslims. In fact, the assistant director in 2020 will be a Muslim who was born and raised in Oberammergau. This will also be the first time the cast has more women than men, and cast members will include people regardless of race and sexual orientation. But the biggest changes have to do with the anti-Semitism in the play.

In the early 1800s a monk from the nearby Ettal monastery revised the Passion Play text which was further developed by his former student who became the parish priest in Oberammergau, Joseph Daisenberger. They made the Passion Play script more biblically accurate and removed elements from popular legend. Instead of pitting Jesus against devilish figures, this script was more human, showing Jesus in conflict with religious authorities. Jewish leaders began to be depicted with hats with horns; this may have resulted from the previous scripts' influence. Regardless, the result of this new script brought new focus on the tension between Jesus and Jewish leadership. As author Helena Waddy observes, "Weis's and Daisenberger's efforts to humanize and biblicize the play had the effect of blaming the Jewish protagonists for its ultimate outcome. Messages of reconciliation and forgiveness were balanced with this depiction of Jewish greed and betrayal. However, this was the biblically sanctioned drama that both players and audiences accepted as true to the Passion story."[5]

Following World War II greater numbers of voices began speaking out against the Oberammergau Passion Play condemning its portrayal of Jews. Prior to the 1970 production the Catholic Church refused to give its official approval known as *missio canonica*. Following that year's performance play organizers invited Jewish groups, including the Anti-Defamation League, to share in script revisions.

Even by the time Stückl took over the play he still felt the need for greater revision. "No one any more wanted to speak about Hitler, but the text was largely there, talking up the intelligence of Pilate and telling you how bad the Jews were. It was scandalous, attracting international attention, and it had to change."[6] Change happened as the story began to be told differently. Otto Huber, a professor of languages and drama, has been a mentor to Stückl. He worked on modernizing the script and presenting Jesus as an observant Jew his whole life. This included such things as Jesus entering the temple and reciting the Shema with the people on stage responding in Hebrew. At the Last Supper a large menorah is on the table and Jesus says Kiddush and Hamotzi, Sabbath blessings, in perfect Hebrew. The disciple John asks, "Why is this night different from all other nights?"

The infamous blood curse has been cleverly omitted. First, Stückl had it spoken amidst the crowd shouting so that the words were not distinguishable. In subsequent years it was removed altogether. Costumes changed so that the hats of religious leaders no longer appeared like horns. Roman soldiers are present throughout the performance clearly establishing their place and authority. And while the high priest is still portrayed as a villain along with Pilate, other dissenting Jewish voices have become prominent.

## Jesus the Master Storyteller

Jesus was a master at telling stories that challenged the popular narratives of his day. One such was told in response to a lawyer's question. The person came up to Jesus with a seemingly sincere desire to know what he must do to have eternal life. Perceiving that the man knew his Scriptures, Jesus asked how the law reads. The lawyer spoke the opening words of the Shema, or "Hear O Israel," from Deuteronomy 6: "You shall love the Lord your God with all your heart, and with all your soul, and with all your strength, and with all your mind; and your neighbor as yourself" (Luke 10:27).

That last part is an addition. Loving your neighbor as yourself is not in the Shema, though it is in the Torah (Leviticus 19:18). Why did this lawyer take it upon himself to combine verses of scripture and tell the story differently? Having heard Jesus speak, this lawyer might have assumed this line of teaching was something Jesus would approve of. But he's left uncomfortable when all Jesus says to him is, "do this and you will live." But then the lawyer responds, "And who is my neighbor?"

Now the lawyer's retort seems a bit snippy, but let's give him the benefit of the doubt. It's actually not a bad question; we need to know who are neighbors and who are strangers. Even so, Jews are commanded to love both, as Leviticus also states. Perhaps he honestly felt he didn't know enough to gain eternal life, that there was something more he needed to learn, and he came to Jesus seeking enlightenment. Maybe he was frustrated by Jesus' answer because it inferred that all he had to do was live out what he already knew. It is like when I go to the doctor and all she tells me is do what I already know: eat right, exercise, and get my rest. I want her to tell me something I don't know, or give me something I don't already have that will make me feel better. Jesus is like my doctor. "Go and do what you already know."

We know this story as the parable of the good Samaritan (Luke 10:25-37). A nameless person without any identifying characteristics traveled between Jerusalem and Jericho, a route known to be dangerous. Not surprisingly he is robbed, beaten, and left for dead. A priest, then separately a Levite, pass by the man.

So far, it's an excellent story. You have intrigue. Who was this man? Why did he choose to go alone on a road known for bandits? You have tension. This man should have known better. Would you say it was his own fault?

Along comes a Samaritan. He goes to the man, realizes he's alive, tends to him and takes him to an inn. He even does the unbelievable act of paying for the innkeeper to look after him, promising to return and pay whatever expenses are left. Who does such a thing?

Now the sting. Jesus asked the lawyer, Who proved to be neighbor to the man who fell among robbers?

Did you get that? The initial question was, "What must I do?" Jesus is now the one asking the questions, and he wants to know who proved to *be*? The lawyer answered, "The one who showed him mercy." He didn't identify him as a Samaritan. Perhaps he couldn't bring himself to say it. Who is my neighbor? Who do I *have* to love in order to inherit eternal life? Anyone. Everyone. The story ends with Jesus telling the lawyer, "Go and do likewise," and that brings us back to doing again! What we do comes from who we are, sort of the old "good root-good fruit" principle.

If you are at all familiar with this thing called church, then you know this story. Pastors and teachers tell us about the historical origins of the Jewish-Samaritan divide. Some even show modern pictures of the road between Jerusalem and Jericho from their latest Holy Land tour. They point out how robbers could easily hide in the rugged mountain terrain.

Like many of Jesus' stories, after learning so much about them, you begin to think the characters were real. Weren't the good Samaritan and the prodigal son actual people? Of course, the answer is no. None of these characters existed. Perhaps the good Samaritan, like many modern movies, was based on a true story, but we don't know that. What we are led to believe is that Jesus made the whole thing up. He took what was real: prejudice, religious intolerance, and false narratives and made up a better story.

Who was this story for? The obvious answer is the lawyer. Jesus told a story in response to his question. But Jesus was clever enough to tell good stories with multiple audiences in mind. I wonder if the story wasn't also (if not more so) for the disciples. Just a few verses earlier (Luke 9:51-55) we read about Jesus and the disciples traveling through a Samaritan village where no one would receive them. They were turned away. James and John were so incensed by the rejection they asked Jesus if they should call down fire from heaven to consume the whole place. Personally, I find that a little harsh, but I guess it depends on your narrative. Instead of rebuking the

Samaritans, though, Jesus rebuked his disciples and they went on their way.

So when just a short time later Jesus tells a story with a Samaritan as the hero I wonder if the ones with gaping jaws would have been the disciples? Like so many other experiences with Jesus, they had to find his behavior confounding. Why would he, fresh on the heels of being turned away by Samaritans, make one of *them* a model neighbor? Could it be that Jesus used fiction in the hope of changing reality?

## Real Fiction

Do you know the name Steve Bartman? If you are a Chicago Cubs baseball fan you probably do. He attended Game 6 of the National League championship at Wrigley Field in 2003. The Cubs were ahead in the series and in that game against the Florida Marlins. They were five outs away from going to the World Series for the first time in forty-eight years. There was huge excitement in the crowd, until a fly ball was hit by a Marlins batter.

Bartman was sitting in the front row on the right field side. He reached up to catch the ball—who wouldn't? What a souvenir to have. But instead of catching it, his arm obstructed the Cubs right fielder who would have made a crucial out in the inning. This started an eight-run inning for the Marlins, who won that game and then the series-deciding game 7. The Cubs once again had to say, "Wait till next season."

For Steve Bartman, however, it probably felt like there was no next season. The crowds yelling at him brought out security people who escorted Bartman out of the stands. As he was led away fans pelted him with objects, cursing him as he went past. He had to be taken to a private room where he remained until the game was over and the crowds completely gone. As the fateful inning continued unfolding, broadcasters kept replaying the moment they said started it all. Death threats were made against Bartman.

He spent the following years living as low profile as he could. He turned down significant offers for interviews and appearances including a six-figure deal to be in a Super Bowl commercial. Now fast forward to 2016. The Cubs at long last won the World Series for the first time in 108 years. Several months later a special ceremony was held to present a World Series ring to Steve Bartman. The Cubs wanted to make right what had been an unfortunate life-changing event. At the ceremony Bartman said this:

> My hope is that we all can learn from my experience to view sports as entertainment and prevent harsh scapegoating, and to challenge the media and opportunistic profiteers to conduct business ethically by respecting personal privacy rights and not exploit any individual to advance their own self-interest or economic gain. Moreover, I am hopeful this ring gesture will be the start of an important healing and reconciliation process for all involved.[7]

Having watched the initial play that tragically changed Bartman's life I was happy for him. But reading his words in the newspaper that day I couldn't help but feel he was talking about more than baseball. With so much division in our world and fear of otherness and temptation to stereotype people by race, religion, and nationality, it seemed like Bartman was talking to all of us. When we see perpetrators and idiots and rednecks and jerks as *people*, our narratives about them change, and so do our actions.

The story reminded me of another recent news event, the twenty-fifth anniversary of the Los Angeles race riots sparked by the acquittal of police officers in the beating of Rodney King. As live news showed the destruction and rioting on televisions throughout the country, one scene was especially haunting. A white truck driver, Reginald Denny, was stopped by rioters who dragged him out of his vehicle and smashed bottles and a brick against his head. Blood streaming down his face, he was dragged into the street and kicked.

The only reason he survived was the actions of four people who came to be known as the Good Samaritans of the LA Riots. Independently these people saw this scene on television and said, "We have to do something. This man needs help." So, they left their homes and arrived on the scene about the same time. They pulled Denny into his truck. The two women started tending to his wounds. One of the men said he could drive while the other stood outside the truck appearing like a rioter so others wouldn't come. They drove to a hospital and were credited for saving Denny's life.

When asked why they, four black people, risked their lives for a white man they didn't know, they said, "We didn't see race. We saw a person and thought, 'What if that was me? What would I hope someone else might do?' So, I did that."[8]

Who proved to be a neighbor? That is what they did.

We can live by narratives that tell us some people deserve what they get. Because some have been mistreated, then mistreatment of others is justified. Some people who make dumb mistakes deserve what they get. My anger and outrage justify my calling down fire from heaven or throwing objects at someone. But without any goodness in the narrative a happy ending is hard to expect.

Sometimes hope lies in fiction. Take a bad incident that infuriates and inflames us and rewrite the script. Imagine the other person not as an evil culprit but a child of God. Imagine what could have possibly made someone created in the image of a loving God to act so unlovingly. Picture the person we despise not as someone hateful, prideful, or selfish, but as they could be, as God made them to be. As Martin Luther King Jr. said, "Darkness cannot drive out darkness; only light can do that. Hate cannot drive out hate; only love can do that."[9] Change the narrative and reality can be changed.

Now this sounds dangerously like forgive and forget. To forget the wrongs that are done is a false narrative in itself. Living as if evil realities did not occur would be as unjust as saying the Holocaust never happened. The only way a story gets better is to recognize the current script needs changing. Recognizing wrongs of the past without letting those wrongs define our future requires courage and faith. Telling a better story means seeing beyond the present and hoping for a future the way God intends. Such hope is what makes tomorrow better.

According to Acts 8, in the aftermath of Stephen's persecution, believers in Jerusalem had to flee the city in search of safety. It says they spread throughout Judea *and Samaria*. Now think about that. If a Samaritan village had once turned away Jesus and his disciples why would his followers have gone there in search of asylum? Could it be that realities were changing? Perhaps because Jesus not only told a better story but also lived it out in the way he treated Samaritans. Samaritans' attitudes toward Jesus' followers changed as a result. Whatever the reason, I'm sure Jesus' disciples were grateful they didn't call down fire from heaven that day.

The parable of the good Samaritan was pure fiction. Jesus confronted tensions in his own community and his own religion and challenged it with a story, a story that had the power to change reality.

There is one more episode to share about the Nazis and Oberammergau. Max-Peter Meyer was the only Jewish resident in Oberammergau in the 1930s. He was known simply as Jud Meyer (Jud is a nickname in German meaning "Jew"). His wife was Aryan, a relationship that would be threatened by the new "Law on the Protection of German Blood," banning sexual relations between Jews and Aryans, even if already married. Such a relationship would be subject to punishment. That may be the reason for what happened one November morning in 1938, just one day after the infamous *Kristall-nacht*, or "Night of Broken Glass." A group of youth from the town stormed into Meyer's home and pulled him outside while doing some damage to his belongings. Shortly after this, Meyer was taken to the concentration camp at Dachau just seventy-five miles away.[10]

Some in the town speculate that the youths were trying to emulate what they heard Nazis in other places had done. Regardless, Meyer disappears from record until nine years later. He appears at the trial of two Oberammergau men accused of being Nazis. One of the men was Alois Lang, who played Jesus in 1930 and 1934, the two years Hitler attended the Passion Play. Lang admitted joining the party in 1938 out of necessity. Without paying the admission fee for party membership Nazi authorities would deny his permit to run a hotel. Though he had resisted for several years, he was now broke and desperate.[11]

Had he been convicted he would have served time in prison. Why was he released? Because of the testimony of Max-Peter

Meyer. Meyer survived Dachau and returned to Oberammergau. When Lang was tried in 1947 Meyer appeared to witness on his behalf. He testified to "the deep friendship and complete acceptance that he had always found in the home of Alois Lang. He emphasized that he would have discerned quickly any Nazi taint there."[12]

As surprising as this turn of events was, what happened next was even more shocking. The other defendant, Aaron Preisinger, took the stand. It was believed he was part of the gang who stormed Meyer's home that November morning. When asked to describe what happened, Meyer confirmed that a group of ten to fifteen men broke into his house, but because they knocked his glasses off, he could not verify exactly who was among them. Without further evidence, Preisinger was released, leaving uncertainty as to just who was among this horde.[13]

Was Meyer truly uncertain as to who was among the group? Even if his glasses had been knocked off could he have not recognized the voices of people he would have known in such a small village? If he did, why wouldn't he have sought to see that they received some punishment for what they did?

We shall never know, but can only speculate if Max-Peter Meyer had tried to tell a better story.

# CHAPTER 6

## THE POWER
## OF THE CROSS

# Chapter 6

# THE POWER
# OF THE CROSS

This idea is new—a live crucifix. We have seen them
in thousands, artistic and inartistic; but we never yet
felt the reality of a man upon a cross.
    *Richard Burton, reflecting on the 1880 Passion Play*

Towering more than 1600 feet above Oberammergau is a
horn-shaped rock outcropping known as the Kofel. Like many
alpine peaks the summit of the Kofel is marked by a large crucifix. The tradition of putting crosses on mountaintops goes
back many centuries in Europe, reflecting the religious inclina-
tions of these strongly Catholic regions. Summit crosses were
often used as boundary markers and in some cases lightning
rods to protect climbers on exposed rock faces. Yet the use of
crosses for such practical purposes speaks to the deep convic-
tions of the people. Putting a cross on a summit was a way to
broadcast faith. But just what is the message being broadcast?

In this chapter we will consider the meaning and significance of the cross and what this enduring symbol of the Christian faith teaches us about God, what it means to be disciples of Christ, and our own experiences of pain and suffering.

The cross is where the tradition of putting on a passion play every ten years in Oberammergau all started. In the midst of their suffering during a plague the people prayed before the crucifix in the parish church. This was not an unusual act. Meditating and praying before the crucifix, particularly in churches or chapels, is a popular practice. As the people prayed for an end to the deaths in their village, they vowed to put on a play telling of Jesus' suffering. The word *passion* comes from the Latin word *passio* meaning "suffering." In their suffering the villagers turned to the suffering of Jesus and found hope. The message they have broadcast for nearly four hundred years is that there is hope in the cross of Christ.

## When Did the Cross Become a Symbol of Christianity?

But just when did the cross become the primary symbol of the Christian faith? Go into most churches anywhere in the world, be they Catholic, Orthodox, or Protestant and you will find crosses of all varieties. Crosses are often worn as necklaces and other jewelry. Cemeteries in many parts of the world are covered with crosses. Crosses have even become popular tattoos. But why? Just when did the cross become *the* Christian symbol?

Historians believe the establishment of the cross as the preeminent symbol of Christian faith evolved over three to four hundred years. In the first centuries of Christian history many symbols were used for the church including the dove, ship, anchor, lyre, and especially fish. The Greek word for fish is *Ichthus* (or *Ichtys*), which Christians used as an acronym that translates to English as "Jesus Christ, Son of God, Savior." What was not as popular a symbol was the cross, and no wonder. The cross was a grotesque image of Roman execution. Touting a cross for a logo would have been the equivalent today of brandishing a guillotine or hangman's noose. Those aren't exactly images one associates with love, grace, and mercy.

Typically, crucifixion was reserved for criminals and rebels, serving not only as a punishment but also as a deterrent. Crucified victims were often left hanging in public places such as roadsides so that passersby, witnessing the awful pain and horror, would be dissuaded from crossing Roman authority. A good example was the uprising led by Spartacus. Hundreds of rebel slaves were crucified and lined along the Appian Way to discourage other slaves from revolting.

A religion that used a cross to identify itself would have been confusing and even horrifying. Yet there is evidence that the cross started to appear as a symbol even in the first few centuries after Jesus' crucifixion. Tertullian, the second-century Christian writer, referenced Christians making the sign of the cross on foreheads. Clement of Alexandria wrote in the early third century how believers made "the Lord's sign," meaning the cross. But perhaps the best confirmation is a gemstone in the British Museum known as "The Magic Crucifix Gem," dating from the late second to early third century. It is the oldest representation of the crucified Jesus in existence, but it gets its name from the writings on the stone thought to be magical incantations.

Many superstitions of the time believed religious symbols

could be used to ward off evil spirits. One place where this could explain the appearance of crosses is Pompeii. Destroyed in AD 79 by a volcanic explosion on Mount Vesuvius, excavations have revealed crosses etched into streets and on walls of buildings. Historian Bruce Longenecker claims these discoveries prove that Christians were indeed in Pompeii, meaning there would have likely been a Christian presence in that city when Paul first came to Italy. Considering, however, the suspicion cast on Christianity following Emperor Nero's blaming of the burning of Rome on Christians in AD 64, it is unlikely that believers would have wanted to be so public with their symbols. Perhaps crosses were prevalent in Pompeii simply because they were a popular emblem of superstitious protection. Regardless of what the crosses meant, it is clear that very early in Christian history, crosses were present.[1]

But it was not until the fourth century that the cross became established as the prevailing emblem of the Christian faith. In AD 325, Emperor Constantine prepared for a battle that would determine the leadership of the Roman Empire. As he prayed for victory he looked into the sky and saw the form of a cross with the words, "Conquer in this." Later that night he had a vision of Jesus explaining the meaning of the cross and directing him to create a banner with a cross formed by the first two Greek letters of "Christ," or the Chi-Rho cross. Constantine won the battle unifying the empire and solidifying his leadership. He converted to Christianity and very quickly the cross became the identifying symbol of the Christian religion. A Biblical Archaeology Society article reports that, "According to fifth-century historian Sozomen, Constantine abolished crucifixion in special reverence for the power and victory he received because of the symbol of the cross."[2]

This history is important because it helps us understand how the cross changed in meaning over these first centuries of Christian faith. Beginning as a symbol of shame and torture with limited recognition, the cross emerged as a symbol of victory, triumph, and cultural popularity. In some ways this development seems good for the church, but in others it sets up a potential false expectation. If one adopts the cross as a symbol of faith then shouldn't it guarantee success and welfare? The contradiction is obvious: a symbol of sacrifice that promises prosperity.

Can you think of ways today people use the cross as a sort of good-luck charm? Can you think of any modern examples where people bring an expectation that their Christian faith should provide them victorious living while sparing them from suffering? The cross will represent an important tension of faith, holding the promise of triumph but through a path of sacrifice. Perhaps this is what led to the creation of the crucifix.

## The Biblical Cross

The disciples were no doubt shocked when Jesus told them, "If any want to become my followers, let them deny themselves and take up their cross and follow me" (Matthew 16:24). There was only one understanding of a cross at that time, and willingly taking one up would have been ludicrous. Without any teaching on the cross specifically by Jesus or reference to his own future death on a cross, what were the disciples to make of his reference?

The Greek word for cross is *stauros*, which simply means upright stake or pole. Some Roman executions were performed by nailing the victim to a single upright pole with hands directly above the head. This led to the speculation that a single pole without a cross beam was a more accurate depiction of the cross on which Jesus was crucified. Other evidence, however, based on drawings of crucifixions at that time, shows arms being stretched outward. Putting these pieces together we can assume that the most common form of crucifixion in the first century started with a stationary upright post. Victims would then carry a beam to these posts, and have their arms affixed to the beam that would then be raised and adjoined to the *stauros*.

One of the earliest symbols of a Christian cross was a *staurogram*, which joined together two letters in Greek, the *tau* and *rho*. This gave the appearance of a stick figure with a head and outstretched arms. In reality this manner of death was excruciating. What often killed those crucified was not being nailed to the beams, but the flogging that happened before and the asphyxiation during. The weight of the body gradually made breathing more difficult. This is also why the arms would have had to be tied to the beams rather than being nailed alone. The body's weight would have pulled the flesh away from the nails. To allow themselves to breathe, victims would push up with their legs as much as they were able. To hasten death, soldiers would sometimes break the legs to make this impossible.

Knowing this reality, how would you have felt if you heard Jesus say you must take up your cross? The image of suffering alone would have been disconcerting to his followers, but the fact that crucifixions were often reserved for the worst of criminals and rebels would have surely made Jesus' command quite baffling. Clearly Jesus isn't talking about being inconvenienced, as if repairing a flat tire is a cross to bear! As well, bearing a cross is not about fulfilling a chosen obligation like caring for an ailing family member. A cross is something you don't choose. Other than committing a violation that merited crucifixion, what could Jesus have meant by this analogy?

### The Humiliation of the Cross

Let's consider a few obvious features of the cross, starting with humiliation. Victims were often stripped completely bare, or on occasion left with nothing but a loincloth. There would have been loss of control over bodily functions, particularly at the moment of death. Thinking of the cross figuratively, Jesus was inviting his followers to endure shame and humiliation, if necessary, as a way of being faithful to God and standing up for others. This humiliation doesn't have to require the physical torture of the cross, but it can mean being put in equally undesirable places.

Former professional baseball player and motivational speaker, John Cassis, tells the story of playing for a minor league team in Shreveport, Louisiana, in the early seventies. John, who is white, had a good friend on that team, Wayne Redmond, who is black. They were both Christians. One day the coach asked John to speak at a church in the community. He agreed and asked his friend Wayne to join him. The coach intercepted John and told him he couldn't do that. When John asked why, the coach explained that it was a white church. So John said, "Well if Wayne can't go, I'm not going."

The next day at the ballpark, John and Wayne, both of whom were regular starters, were scratched from the lineup. As the team ran out to take the field, Wayne grabbed his glove before anyone could stop him and took his usual position in the outfield. A fly ball was hit to him, but he never tried to catch it. He let the ball drop at his feet. Another outfielder ran to pick up the ball and throw it to the infield, screaming at Wayne as he did. The coach stopped the game and sent in a replacement for Wayne who was booed furiously by the crowd as he walked off the field. Right before he stepped into the dugout a fan poured a beer over his head. As he walked past John, the two slyly touched gloves. The next day John would learn that his friend was no longer with the team.

No one in the stands had any idea that day why Wayne Redmond let a ball drop. They probably assumed the worst about his motives, feeling he let the team and them down. They derided him.[3]

When Jesus told his disciples to carry a cross he wasn't saying we should literally be crucified. He was saying that following him means being willing to be misunderstood, wrongly judged, and derided. In short, carrying a cross involves enduring humiliating places. Such a place may result from taking a stand like Wayne Redmond or lowering ourselves to do humbling chores in order to show love to others. Maybe such a place will come from the honest admission of sins we have committed. Some people look at humility as weakness, but facing humiliation always requires courage.

### The Sacrifice of the Cross

The cross also represented sacrifice. Clearly it was an instrument of death. Correlating a cross to the Christian life meant being willing to die to self in order to give life in some manner to others. As Stephen Covey said, "Sacrifice is giving up something good for something better."[4]

This past year a woman from India named Mandeep wandered into our church one evening. My wife noticed her thumbing through information about the church and asked if she could help. Within a few minutes Mandeep was pouring out her heart. After suffering chronic pain and fatigue for several years she had finally been diagnosed with an autoimmune disease that was destroying her kidneys. Without a transplant she would not live long. She was on a registry but was so far down the list she didn't have much hope of finding a donor in time.

That Sunday she came to church and I met her after the service. She said, "I know this is crazy, but if you know anyone willing to donate a kidney, I could use it!" I thought, *I can't remember anyone telling me lately they have a spare kidney to give*, but I assured her that I would see what I could do.

In my weekly e-mail to the church the following Friday I encouraged people to consider being organ donors and explained that there has never been a better time. I mentioned Mandeep's need and said that if anyone felt led to investigate this gift of life to let us know at the church. About a month before Christmas, and nearly eight months after that e-mail, I walked by a staff member's office. She said excitedly, "Did you hear Mandeep located a donor?" I had not. As it turns out a retired woman in the church contacted Mandeep. She was tested and found that she wasn't a suitable donor. But she mentioned to her adult daughter, a medical doctor, what she had done and the daughter asked for more information. What the mother did not know is that her daughter had recently had a peculiar dream. She went to heaven and was asked what good things she had done in her life. After giving several answers, she was asked, "But why didn't you give a kidney? You had a chance to donate a kidney and did not." She awoke from the dream startled, wondering what it meant.

And here, days later, she heard from her mother about

a woman from India desperately needing a kidney and suddenly her dream was making sense. The two women met one
evening and the daughter felt even more compelled to investigate the possibility of donating one of her kidneys. She was
tested and found to be a suitable candidate. Four days before
Christmas I met the two women in the surgical preparation
room where they joined hands as we prayed together. The
surgery was a success and both patients are doing great. For
the daughter, the experience has been a deeply spiritual one,
filling her with a joy from knowing God used her to give life
to someone else.

### The Salvation of the Cross

One final observation about the figurative meaning of
the cross is that it is a symbol of salvation. Through the cross
Christians have come to find assurance of forgiveness and
reconciliation with God. This belief is called *atonement,* one
of the more debated theological ideas in the church. In fact,
because of the disparity of opinion over the understanding of
atonement, there has yet to be an official doctrine of atonement in Christianity.

At the heart of the debate is whether God needed to
have a sacrifice in order to forgive. Going back to the sacrificial system of the Old Testament, some find that in the
cross Jesus became a new Passover lamb. Instead of offering
our own sacrifice for deliverance, God makes the offering for
us. Others, however, contend that this paints an unsettling
image of God, as one who must be paid in order to forgive,
even if God makes the payment himself. Different theories
of the atonement present Jesus as a substitution for our sacrifice, a ransom paid to the devil, and a moral example or

influence. The pitfalls of each explain why there is no single accepted theory.

While we will not settle the questions of atonement here, let's agree that as a symbol of salvation many Christians believe that the cross represents God's power and desire to take all the damage and costs created by human sin and absorb the loss himself. This would be like visiting someone in their home and breaking a vase that is more valuable than we can repay. Even though we are told not to worry about paying for the vase, we know the owner is absorbing the loss. A price is still paid.

Harry Emerson Fosdick said in his sermon, "The Forgiveness of Sin,"

> I do not know what theory of the atonement you may
> hold, and I might also say I don't care whether you
> have any theory at all, but recognize this fact: behind
> all the explanations of atonement that have arisen and
> taken form and faded away in the history of Christian thought this conviction has lain deep—the cross
> means that it was not easy for God to forgive. It cost.[5]

Captured in the meaning of the cross is the idea that God has done something more wonderful than we could ever do for ourselves. We are restored to right relationship with God. We don't have to make up for all the things that got the relationship out of line. This is the work of grace, but grace means more than just wiping the slate clean. It means we can write a new story. In accepting that our lives have been redeemed by a divine life, we want to live for the Redeemer. We are filled with gratitude and a desire to live a redeemed life. Perhaps this is why Catholics started putting Jesus back on the cross.

## Crucifix vs. Plain Cross

The oldest known image of Jesus' crucifixion is a wood carving on the doors of the Basilica of Santa Sabina in Rome dating to the fifth century, at least two hundred years after Constantine saw his victorious cross in the sky. This is believed to be the first crucifix, which means "one fixed to a cross." By this time people no longer associated the cross with the ghastly images of crucifixion, but it's a curious question as to why this many years after Christianity was adopted by the Roman Empire that Jesus' body began appearing on crosses. Could it be that following Constantine's adoption of Christianity, the cross became politically correct and was associated with victory and success while the understanding of redemption, sacrifice, and humiliation was getting lost? Perhaps concerned church leaders began putting images of Jesus' suffering body on the cross to remind worshippers of the nature of God's love and the kind of love his followers are called to emulate.

Whatever the reason for the emergence of crucifixes—the representation of Christ on the cross—they became significant for the practice of faith. Some Christians are encouraged to pray and meditate in front of a crucifix. A crucifix must be present in the performance of Mass so as to recognize the sacrifice of Christ reenacted in the service. Believers are encouraged to place crucifixes in their homes. Nearly a thousand years later, many Protestants would return to a plain cross mainly to distinguish themselves from Catholics but also to focus on the victory of resurrection. Catholics today would say the crucifix emphasizes the Resurrection while also emphasizing the path by which Resurrection came. I believe there is a place and need for both in our worship. Too often a plain cross, on the one hand, so emphasizes the victory of the Resurrection that we end up avoiding the reality of suffering. The crucifix, on the other hand, helps us hold together the great dichotomy of faith: suffering and hope.

## Suffering and Hope (or God's Suffering and Ours)

On the last year of every decade, one year before the next Passion Play season, Oberammergau puts on a production called *Die Pest*, or The Plague. It recalls the pestilence that struck the village and led to their vow made in 1633. It is a way for the community to remember why they do what they are about to do. The play had been performed unchanged since its creation in 1933 until Christian Stückl was asked to direct it in 1988. One major change was an added scene involving a number of youth. Stückl was aware that increasing numbers of young people were open and honest about their lack of faith. So, he has them capture the struggles of the ancient villagers while giving voice to their modern doubts. They gather around a large crucifix on the stage and hurl it to the ground saying they can't believe in a God who allows such suffering.[6]

While the scene was scandalous to many in the audience, Stückl was simply expressing a disconnect felt by many through the centuries. How can God permit pain? One of the earliest historical examples of this struggle is revealed by graffiti found on the wall of a building in Rome that housed slaves in the third century. There is an image of a human body with a donkey head with arms outstretched as if being crucified. Below it is a Roman slave raising an arm as if worshipping. The caption reads, "Alexemenos worships god." Most likely it is one slave mocking another named Alexemenos who was a Christian. Even then the idea of worshipping a God who suffered crucifixion was inconceivable, at least to those who didn't understand. For early Christians however, there seems to be a paradoxical hope found in a God who doesn't remove suffering but shares it.

In the introduction to his book *Walking with God Through Pain and Suffering,* Tim Keller talks about sitting with people who have gone through tragedies that cause them to reject God and turn away from their faith. "But at the same time," he writes, "I learned that just as many people *find* God through affliction and suffering. They find that adversity moves them toward God rather than away."[7]

One can take away much from reading the Bible, and a great lesson it is that suffering is not covered up or pushed aside, particularly in the lives of believers. Centuries of suffering for God's people led to their deliverance under Moses. Nowhere are we told why they suffered so long, only that God eventually brought them to a better place—not in spite of their suffering but as a result of it. Later we learn how the apostasy of God's people led to their destruction at the hands of the Babylonians. In returning from exile the prophets promised that in being faithful they would have prosperity. But what about those who are faithful and still suffer, such as the patriarchs and matriarchs of Genesis? Or Job, or Mary the mother of Jesus? In the New Testament we learn that the deaths of Christians caused a crisis of faith in the church. They were led to believe that Jesus would return in their lifetimes and set right all that was out of order. Therefore, Peter wrote to assure them, "Dear friends, don't be surprised at the fiery trials you are going through, as if something strange were happening to you" (1 Peter 4:12 NLT). From beginning to end the Bible declares that suffering is not contrary to faith but a part of it, and this truth is symbolized in the cross.

The cross assures us that tragedy, no matter how tragic, is never terminal. In 1942 a terrible fire burned the popular Cocoanut Grove Night Club in Boston. Nearly five hundred people died. It was clearly the kind of tragedy that would make one say "nothing good can come of this." And yet in spite of the suffering some found pathways to hope.

The cross declares God's authority over the evil of the world because God transforms rather than eradicates evil. For many of us, eradicating evil seems like a better plan, but what else would be removed as well? What would be lost if we lose the ability to choose between good and evil? What would be lost if our freedom to choose our response to suffering was taken? What would become of love if there was never anything unloving? It is through pain that we come to want with greater desire that which is good and pure and loving. Our hope either hides in or is hidden by our wants.

Dr. John Wimmer is a United Methodist pastor and friend. Last year he published a book, *Blessed Endurance: Moving Beyond Despair to Hope*.[8] John knows something of which he writes. Years ago, he and his wife, Jan, were expecting twins. Twenty-four weeks into the pregnancy, complications forced an early delivery. One child died and the other survived but not without lengthy hospitalizations and permanent disability. John speaks of his trust in Paul's admonition that God works for good in everything. He believes those words are true and that is what gives him hope.

Just as his book was going to print, I got a call at the church one day informing me that John was in the emergency room. He had not been feeling well and after a battery of tests learned he had a very rare form of small cell cancer. His prognosis was not good but his and Jan's hope propelled them forward. They immediately located doctors with specialization in this type of cancer, identified a method of treatment, and began a fight that has been full of highs and lows over the past eighteen months. Even as I write these words, I think of seeing him in church the day before, smiling, hoping, and fighting. What keeps him going? A silly, crazy idea that God works through suffering, not around it. Before his book was published, he wrote an epilogue in which he said,

> Now it is time for me to learn again how to live into the words I have written. I must rely on the honesty and promises of the scriptures I have quoted, look to Jesus on the cross as God's expression of suffering love and oneness with me and all who are in pain or despair, avail myself of the Christian faith's treasury of wisdom that has been passed down for generations about how to deal with life's trials, master my pride alone without guides or assistance, embrace humility in admitting my need to accept help in this time of affliction, and above all, practice the undervalued virtue of Christian endurance—the power that overflows from the hope of the Resurrection, that overcomes the grip of disease, trauma, pain, despair, and grief in this life and that has ultimately conquered death itself. In looking back over a final edit of my own words during the last troubling week, I am struck by the fact that I still believe every word.[9]

There is no relieving the tension that pain can separate us from God, yet there is no denying the testimony of many who affirm the belief that "neither death, nor life . . . nor anything else in all creation, will be able to separate us from the love of God in Christ Jesus our Lord" (Romans 8:38-39).

I. Lilias Trotter was a renowned English painter in the early twentieth century. In a time when women were believed not to possess outstanding artistic skill, she broke down barriers. She was a devout Christian and after hearing the evangelist Dwight Moody preach, she responded to a call to become a missionary. She left her art career and spent the next forty years of her life in northern Africa. In her book *Parables of the Cross* she wrote these words, "Take the very hardest thing in your life—the place of difficulty, outward or inward, and expect God to triumph gloriously in that very spot. Just there He can bring your soul into blossom."[10]

Such truths are not learned in leisure. Such hope is not found in the experience of victory. The hope of the cross comes in meeting the Crucified Lord in the crucible of life's trials and finding his presence that sustains us. That helps us believe that good can be erected from the wreckage and gives us faith that we do not walk such lonely paths alone.

The first forty years of the Oberammergau Passion Play were performed in the cemetery where the eighty-four members of the village had been buried. In the place of their grief they lifted up the story of the one who came to bear our griefs and sorrows. In the place of death, they told of a Savior who died for us. They praised God for the hope they found in telling the story of the cross.

On my last evening in Oberammergau I spent time in the cemetery beside the parish church. Along the church wall is a life-size crucifix lifted eight or ten feet from the ground. Jesus' head leans down as if bearing the weight of all the world's sin and agony of the moment. His eyes are open and standing beneath that cross you feel as if he is looking straight at you. Not being accustomed to crucifixes, I found the experience very moving. I could not help but be transfixed by the feeling that Jesus was looking directly at me. No one else was around. I felt as though Jesus were saying, "You are worthy of my love and I share every burden of your life." I could understand in those few quiet moments why meditating and praying before a crucifix can be such a powerful experience. This is a place I would want to visit in a difficult time to be reminded that Christ helps bear my pain and struggles. I understood with new meaning why we call the story of Jesus' suffering the Passion.

# NOTES

## Introduction

1. "Social Consequences of the Thirty Years' War: Was It Worth It?" Ancient Origins (website), September 26, 2017, www .ancient-origins.net/history-important-events/social -consequences-thirty-years-war-was-it-worth-it-008850.

## Chapter 1

1. "History of the Passion Play," Nature Park Ammergau Alps (website), last modified March 27, 2019, www.ammergauer -alpen.de/oberammergau/en/Discover-History-and-stories /Passion-Play/History-of-the-Passion-Play.
2. Michael Counsell, "Historical Notes: A Promise Kept for 366 Years in Oberammergau," *Independent* (website), December 9, 1999, www.independent.co.uk/news/people/historical-notes-a -promise-kept-for-366-years-in-oberammergau-1131213.html.
3. Howard E. Covington Jr., *Making Disciples for Christ: A Businessman's Passion for His Church* (Greensboro, N.C.: Howard E. Covington Jr., 2006), 40–41.
4. *The Lord of the Rings: The Fellowship of the Ring*, directed by Peter Jackson, 2001, New Line Cinema.

5. Victor Hugo, *Les Misérables*, Chapter XIII. The Bishop Works, The Literature Network (website), www.online-literature.com /victor_hugo/les_miserables/26/.

# Chapter 2

1. Bob Smith, "Never Cry Over Anything That Can't Cry Over You," Guide Posts with Bob Smith (blog), December 5, 2013, https://guidepostswithbobsmith.com/2013/12/page/3/.
2. James Shapiro, "Updating (and Retouching) an Old Passion Play," *New York Times*, May 12, 2000, http://movies2 .nytimes.com/books/00/07/09/specials/shapiro-play.html.
3. Weber Shandwick Report, *Civility in America VII: The State of Civility*, www.webershandwick.com/uploads/news/files /Civility_in_America_the_State_of_Civility.pdf.
4. Fred R. Rogers (speech, Marquette University, Milwaukee, WI, given at presentation of honorary degree: Doctor of Letters Conferred on Fred Rogers, May 2001), www.marquette.edu /universityhonors/honors_rogers_speech.shtml.
5. Tod Bolsinger, *Canoeing the Mountains: Christian Leadership in Uncharted Territory* (Downer's Grove, IL: InterVarsity, 2015), 78.
6. John R. Mott, *Cooperation and the World Mission* (Concord, N.H.: Rumford, 1935), 9–10.
7. Stan Copeland, "Room for All" (sermon, Uniting Methodists Conference, July 16, 2018).

# Chapter 3

1. James Shapiro, "Updating (and Retouching) an Old Passion Play," *New York Times*, May 12, 2000, http://movies2.nytimes .com/books/00/07/09/specials/shapiro-play.html.
2. Charles Duhigg, *The Power of Habit: Why We Do What We Do in Life and Business* (New York: Random House, 2012), 19.
3. Duhigg, 212.
4. Duhigg, 235.

5. Francesca Gino and Michael I. Norton, "Why Rituals Work," *Scientific American*, May 14, 2003, www.scientificamerican .com/article/why-rituals-work/.

# Chapter 4

1. James Shapiro, "Updating (and Retouching) an Old Passion Play," *New York Times*, May 12, 2000, http://movies2.nytimes .com/books/00/07/09/specials/shapiro-play.html.
2. Michael White, "Behind the Scenes at the World's Most Celebrated Passion Play," *Catholic Herald*, November 22, 2019, https://catholicherald.co.uk/magazine/you-can-really-feel -who-jesus-was/.
3. James Shapiro, *Oberammergau: The Troubling Story of the World's Most Famous Passion Play* (New York: Random House, 2000), 6.
4. Shapiro, 134.
5. *All the Way*, directed by Jay Roach (2016 HBO Films).
6. Nicholas Kulish, "Church Crisis Shakes Faith of German Town," *New York Times*, May 14, 2010, https://www.nytimes.com /2010/05/15/world/europe/15germany.html.
7. Timothy Keller, *Encounters with Jesus: Unexpected Answers to Life's Biggest Questions* (New York: Penguin Books, 2013), 69.
8. Kulish, "Church Crisis Shakes Faith."
9. Michael Counsell, *Every Pilgrim's Guide to Oberammergau and Its Passion Play*, 2nd rev. ed. (London: Canterbury Press, Norwich, 2008).
10. *Validation*, directed by Kurt Kuenne, Theater Junkies, 2007, https://www.youtube.com/watch?v=Cbk980jV7Ao.

# Chapter 5

1. Helena Waddy, *Oberammergau in the Nazi Era: The Fate of a Catholic Village in Hitler's Germany* (New York: Oxford University Press, 2010), 135.
2. James Shapiro, *Oberammergau: The Troubling Story of the*

*World's Most Famous Passion Play* (New York: Random House, 2000), 149.

3. "The Passion Play of Oberammergau," Catholic Arrogance (website), http://catholicarrogance.org/Catholic /Oberammergau.html.

4. Michael White, "Behind the Scenes at the World's Most Celebrated Passion Play," *Catholic Herald*, November 22, 2019, https://catholicherald.co.uk/magazine/you-can-really-feel -who-jesus-was/.

5. Waddy, *Oberammergau in the Nazi Era*, 18.

6. White, "Behind the Scenes."

7. "Cubs Issue World Series Ring to Notorious Fan Bartman," AP News, July 31, 2017, www.apnews.com/6725c07f05d14371b 45634ce0f0b22a4.

8. Mary Harris, "Good Samaritan Remembers the LA Riots 20 Years Later," NBC Los Angeles (website), April 23, 2012, www.nbclosangeles.com/news/local/A-Good-Samaritan -Remembers--148613585.html.

9. Martin Luther King Jr., *Strength to Love* (Minneapolis: Augsburg Fortress, 2010), 47.

10. Shapiro, *Oberammergau*, 142–46.

11. Kathleen McLaughlin, "Alois Lang, Christus, Wins Mercy as Ex-Nazi on Testimony of Jews; Principal in Oberammergau Passion Play Fined After Pleading Coercion at Trial—Anton Preisinger Also Let Off," *New York Times*, May 28, 1947, www .nytimes.com/1947/05/28/archives/alois-lang-christus-wins -mercy-as-exnazi-on-testimony-of-jews.html.

12. Shapiro, 174.

13. Shapiro, 174.

# Chapter 6

1. Bruce W. Longenecker, *The Crosses of Pompeii: Jesus-Devotion in a Vesuvian Town* (Minneapolis: Fortress, 2016).

2. Steven Shisley, "Jesus and the Cross," *Bible History Daily*, Biblical Archaeology Society, March 26, 2018, www.biblical

archaeology.org/daily/biblical-topics/crucifixion/jesus-and
-the-cross/.

3. John Cassis, personal communication with author, February 27, 2019.

4. Stephen R. Covey, *The 8th Habit: From Effectiveness to Greatness* (New York: Simon & Schuster, 2006), 79.

5. Harry Emerson Fosdick and Henry Pitney Van Dusen, *Riverside Sermons* (New York: Harper and Brothers, 1958), 298.

6. James Shapiro, *Oberammergau: The Troubling Story of the World's Most Famous Passion Play* (New York: Random House, 2000), 196.

7. Timothy Keller, *Walking with God through Pain and Suffering* (New York: Penguin, 2015), 5.

8. John R. Wimmer, *Blessed Endurance: Moving Beyond Despair to Hope* (Nashville: Upper Room Books, 2018).

9. Wimmer, 107.

10. I. Lilias Trotter, *Parables of the Cross* (n.p.: SMK, 2013), 8.

\*\*\*\*\*\*\*\*\*\*\*\*\*\*\*\*\*\*\*\*\*\*\*\*\*\*\*\*\*\*\*\*\*\*\*\*\*\*\*\*

# Educational Opportunities Tours

I would like to thank Educational Opportunities Tours (EO) for their support of the work and travel that made this book possible.

Since 1974, Educational Opportunities has been dedicated to providing quality Christian travel programs at an affordable price. Over the years, more than 400,000 Christians have traveled on the various faith-based tours. For more than fifteen years, the staff at EO have worked with our Abingdon Press authors, and their advice and support have helped us invite you, the reader, along for journeys to religious sites in places such as the Holy Land, the British Isles, Turkey, Greece, Italy, Egypt, and Germany.

For more information, go to www.eo.TravelWithUs.com.